I SPONSORED
A CHILD.

HOLT INTERNATIONAL

SHE IS MINE

A WAR ORPHAN'S INCREDIBLE JOURNEY OF SURVIVAL

STEPHANIE FAST

D & S PUBLISHING
Aloha, Oregon

She Is Mine
is dedicated to
the 143,000,000 orphans in the world.

These children will probably never have voices loud enough or public enough to share their life journeys with you. My hope is that this book will become their voice as well as mine. Yes, this book is about my orphan memories, but it is also about the many other orphans in the world. Names, places, and times change, but the challenges of being an orphan—or a vulnerable child—anywhere in the world are very real, very difficult, and generally much the same.

She Is Mine is also dedicated to all who have committed their lives to being a voice for the parentless and all children at risk. It is frightening to think how different my own life might have been if not for heroes like you.

When I walk into the thick of trouble,
  keep me alive in the angry turmoil...
Save me.
Finish what you started in me, GOD.
Your love is eternal—don't quit on me now.

—the Psalmist (MSG)

Contents

PART 3

Acknowledgments

A host of people have filled me to overflowing with thankfulness. I want each of you to know how grateful I am. My blessing toward you is that you would experience the rich love of your Father, that you would hear his applause and his shout of "Great job!"

To my mom and dad, David and Judy Merwin: Thank you for your ability to look beyond the limitations of human sight and to believe that the Spirit of God was telling you to take me home and raise me as your daughter. Your belief in me and your continual love have grounded me. Thank you for instilling in me the hope that there was a future and destiny ahead.

Darryl, you've loved me forever. You've never wavered. You have been constant, covering me with your patient leading. Through impossibilities, you held my hand and kept my heart safe as we built our own family. Thank you for walking in our destiny.

Stephen and Davin, you hold my heart! Each time I look at you, I know that what man says is impossible,

God says is possible. You filled our home with laughter and tears! Thank you for being a part of my destiny. You brought your wives and our wonderful grandchildren into the family, filling our lives with so much extra love.

Catherine and Charlie Johnson, you have been deep and solid life-givers. You walked with me through so many prayers and buckets of tears as this book took form. Your family gave up many hours of family time to support the writing of *She Is Mine*. This book has a destiny because of the many ways in which you have given to it.

Kristie and Dan DeHaven, your time away from your family, your creative touch in writing, your friendship, and your belief have influenced us to believe in a destiny for this book.

Our board members, your prayers, encouragement, and input have been so valuable. Thank you for enabling this book to bring hope to orphans around the world.

Ed Schwartz, thank you for listening to the Lord and for the hours you dedicated to helping write the first draft of this book. I will be forever grateful.

John and Lyza Clarke, you have been friends for many years. Thank you for loving me, counseling me, and being a part of my healing process. You are a part of our destiny.

Thanks to Dave Lambert, the best editor, and to John Topliff and Somersault for your expertise and amazing vision. Your talents show through in this book. Thanks for being a part of this destiny.

My All in All, you have encouraged me, fought for me, pruned me, given me an identity, made me legitimate, given me purpose, and healed me so that I can trust. My destiny is full of joy and hope because of you. The words *thank you* sound so weak—but you know my heart! People sometimes ask me, "How can you be so transparent, sharing all the ugliness that has happened to you, all the dashed hopes?" My only answer is, "I am so grateful for what he has done for me, how can I not do what he has asked me to do?"

Preface

This story follows the path of my life as a child of destiny.

Most people have memories linked together like a film with no end because the gaps are filled in by others in their lives. My memories have been like a slide show—still pictures with empty spaces between—until the writing of this book forced me to remember and fill in the gaps and correct or clarify my memories. They are all I have, and they are precious to me. As you read, I believe that you will be mostly able to discern where I have filled in the gaps to create a seamless history.

Since I have not been able to remember my birth name, I have chosen *Yoon Myoung*, which translates as *Destiny*.

You will notice that, although the story is mine, recounting what happened directly to me, it is written in the third person. There is a reason. While this is the story of my life, it differs only in cultural details from the stories of the innumerable nameless and faceless orphans around the world today. This story belongs to the world's other orphans as much as it belongs to me, and I did not want to disguise that truth in a first-person narrative.

PART 1

CHAPTER 1

The American Soldier

Friday afternoon, December 25, 1953—Christmas Day

He was a tall, lean, twenty-two-year-old, a world away from home. The creases on his face had not been there two years earlier. A jagged scar on his left cheek, just above the jawline, would forever remind him that he had survived when so many others had not. Despite five months of cease-fire, shadows hung in his eyes as he trudged along the rock-hard dirt road.

Nearly two years had passed since the day he had kicked off his farm boots to collapse in a kitchen chair, exhausted from working in the Montana wheat fields. The spring wheat he and his father had planted months earlier, working side by side, had turned a golden yellow, perfect for harvest. As he reached across the table for the pitcher of water, he noticed an envelope on the table—addressed to him. He felt his skin turn cold and his stomach twist. He knew immediately what was in that envelope: his worst fears brought to reality.

Hands trembling, he carried the envelope to his room.

He pulled his folding knife from his pocket and opened it. Slowly, he slid the blade into the small gap in the envelope, sliced it open, and dropped onto his bed.

The letter began, "Order to Report for Induction."

After hearing his brother's stories of World War II, the young man had no desire to relive the life of his soldier brother. His stare shifted to the date stamp on the letter— he had been given less than a month.

His heart pounded heavily as he gazed first at his baseball trophies, then out the window. His mind spun. Fear and anxiety gripped him—and anger, welling up from deep inside. *Where is this place Korea? What are they fighting about? My parents—how long will it be until I see them again? Mom's heart will be broken. Will I smell this sweet fragrance of growing wheat again? Will she wait for me?*

The nearly month-long ship ride to the port of Pusan, on the southeastern tip of the Korean peninsula, gave him long days and nights to contemplate what lay ahead. When he arrived, truth set in quickly. South Korea was a country marked by chaos.

In the aftermath of World War II, the Korean peninsula was divided along the 38th parallel. To the north was communist North Korea, and to the south, the anticommunist Republic of South Korea. On June 25, 1950, the North had invaded the South, leading to the outbreak of the Korean War. This war, often known as the "forgotten war," ended after three horrible years with the signing of the Korea Armistice Agreement in July 1953, in Panmunjom.

Now, just a few months after that signing, the young man walking this hard South Korean road desperately wanted to forget this war forever. He despised his memories. He could still see the despair on the faces of refugees pushing south, their meager possessions on their backs. Bodies along the side of the road, frozen by the bone-chilling winter—and during the sweltering summer months, those bodies created a repulsive stench that could not be avoided. He hated the constant, distant explosion of bombs and the rapid flashes of rifle fire. Two years of this devastation had brought a heavy darkness to his spirit. His youth had been drained. Montana and his boyhood dreams had been stolen from him.

In this dismal aftermath of war, his unit, along with others from the army and the U.N., were assigned to try to bring back some degree of sanity and appearance of normalcy to South Korea. Despite the cease-fire, he was weary.

A light sprinkling of snow covered the outskirts of Pusan. The village had sprung up to do business with the military base. He glanced at his watch—he had an entire afternoon to kill before getting back to the base. But he had needed to escape his buddies in the noisy and bustling USO. They couldn't reach his deep-seated loneliness or heal the anguish he felt in his heart. His friends had their own stories—their own traumas and demons to fight. His felt different and intensely personal, and he had needed to get away for a while—although he was looking forward to the USO's Christmas show that evening, with a troupe from America performing Christmas carols.

He walked past the chain-link fence that marked the base's boundary. He knew the fence was there, in part, to protect him, but lately he'd felt as if it was there to imprison him.

The small village sat less than a hundred yards away. The rutted dirt alley that led toward it was all too familiar. Normally, there would be a seductively dressed woman near the gate, calling out enticingly, expecting to earn a small amount of money. He was thankful that on this day, no one appeared, and he could walk the path unnoticed.

He imagined Christmas Day with his family in Montana. He smiled as he thought about his younger sister opening her gifts and about Christmas dinner with all the trimmings: turkey, cranberries, potatoes and gravy, green beans, and his favorite—apple pie. The thought of relaxing in front of a crackling fire, listening to the snores of his yellow Lab curled up at his feet, almost warmed his tired, frigid body as he walked slowly down the road. Then a blast of arctic air brought him quickly back to reality. He wanted to be home on Christmas Day, not alone in this desolate country. It was almost more than his fragile emotions could handle. He felt empty. He hated how the loneliness enveloped him, but he couldn't shake it.

Absorbed in his thoughts and unaware of how far he had traveled, he felt the sudden sensation of being watched. He looked up.

Her head was lowered, her eyes downcast. She stood behind a rough wooden fence in the dark shadows of the alley beside one of the small stores, which also served as a home for its owners. Partly hidden by a water barrel, she seemed to be watching him. Dressed as she was in heavy winter clothing, it was hard for him to discern how old she was, but he guessed she was about his age.

He slowed slightly, watching her from beneath his cap.

Apparently startled, she averted her eyes. He was touched by her shyness, and he glanced away, unwilling to embarrass her.

After such a hard and cruel war, how could anyone still have the capacity to be soft and timid? Most girls in the base village would have called out to him. And most soldiers would have eagerly responded. But he wasn't like most soldiers, and she didn't seem to behave like most of the girls. He was curious. He glanced back and caught her peering around the corner of the house at him. She quickly pulled back when she saw him looking.

Intrigued, he turned and slowly retraced his steps.

CHAPTER 2

Sook Hee

It had been a strenuous day of work for Sook Hee. Rising before the first glimpse of morning sun, she had made her way to the base cafeteria to help prepare meals for hundreds of hungry American soldiers.

"I don't want to do this today," she sighed as she walked to work, exhausted but aware that it was a privilege to have this job. What if fate had called her to dishonor her family like so many other girls her age, who were selling their bodies in the base village?

"Thanks, pretty lady," soldiers would say each day as they placed their empty dishes on the counter. She never looked directly at them, but she could feel their eyes lingering on her.

"What are you doing when you get off tonight?" others would ask, and a feeling of nakedness and embarrassment would come over her.

If only they would not speak to me, Sook Hee thought.

There was one soldier, though, whose infrequent words and quiet smiles she did not mind. He never said anything other than, "Thank you. Everything was very good." His smile was slight and never embarrassed her or made her feel threatened. But his smiles never reached his eyes, which were so sad. She found that she actually looked forward to seeing him.

After dinner came the task of washing the endless piles of dishes. While making the countless trips to fill wooden buckets with water from the well, she would think about the sorrows of the previous years.

The memory of the sudden death of her parents two years earlier still created an inescapable grief. That day, she had wandered out of the house she shared with her parents and approached the wooden gate—a false symbol of security from the chaos of war on the outside. Her mother had sent her to fetch her father from the fields so that he could return home for a hot midday meal of *doenjang jigae*, Korean bean-paste stew. Sook Hee softly sang her way out into the field, a deliberate attempt to shut out the ugliness of the war-torn world outside.

But before she could reach her father, a deafening blast and blinding light forced her to her knees. She instinctively ducked and covered her head. After a moment, when some of the shock had worn off, she stumbled to her feet, confused and disoriented, and rushed back toward home.

"No!" she cried, seeing the pile of rubble their house had been reduced to. Her mother was now buried somewhere beneath that pile.

She hid weeping in a ditch until the bombing ceased, then returned to the field—and found her father's lifeless body.

It was all just a memory now, frozen by her hard life: Laughing with her parents while sitting on floor pillows around the low kitchen table, playing *baduk* with her father, making *kimchee* with her mother—combining just the right amounts of cabbage, onions, garlic, and spices before placing it in earthenware jars for the winter burial and fermentation process. Those memories now simply reminded her of her loneliness, grief, and loss.

A voice jolted her back to reality. "Sook Hee, pay attention to what you are doing and get busy!"

Water had spilled from her bucket. She swiftly mopped up the mess and continued with her assigned tasks. The sooner she finished, the sooner she could escape to her rented room a short distance from the base.

Many small businesses—food stands, clothing stalls, tailor shops, and the like—slowly developed along the alleyways outside the base. The owners of these shops, whose homes were in the back, would sometimes have an extra room for someone in need. Sook Hee was thankful for the older couple, friends of her parents, who had opened a small pharmacy not far from the base. They allowed her to move into their extra room. While thankful for this warm place to sleep, she often felt alone and vulnerable.

Since the death of her parents, she had lived each day in terror of death, of pain, of injury. When she was not serving at the military base, Sook Hee kept mostly to herself.

When her workday ended, Sook Hee bundled herself for the ten-minute walk home. She would have loved nothing more than to hurry to her room in the village and collapse, but she still had her evening meal and chores to attend to. As she walked, taking in the brisk winter air, she resisted the temptation of self-pity. *At least I still have family*, Sook Hee reminded herself, *even though they live in another village. So many people around me have lost everyone. I could go live with my uncle's family if this becomes too much.*

In Sook Hee's culture, family was a priceless commodity. Parents, in their old age, would always be taken in and cared for by the eldest son in the family, which made the first male child of extreme value. If they didn't have a son, their oldest daughter would take them in after she married. But in her family, her uncle—her father's older brother—was the oldest son, and her grandparents lived with him and his family.

Sook Hee would have to seek out her family before long, anyway, now that the war was over. Like many Korean young people, she had been betrothed while still a young child to one of the sons in the Kim family—a good match. But the war had disrupted all personal matters such as betrothals and marriage, and Sook Hee did not know whether her betrothed had survived the war. Her uncle would have to make inquiries on her behalf.

When she arrived home, Sook Hee went to the water barrel alongside the house for water for her barley and tea. As she reached out to break the layer of ice on the surface, resigned to spending another lonely night in her room, she was startled by the crunch of frozen gravel. She looked up and saw a lone American soldier walking along the dirt alleyway. She recognized him as the kind, sad-eyed soldier from the base, and her heart jumped. She watched him with cautious curiosity. Why was he out alone, and not back at the club with the other soldiers? Was he looking for female companionship, a woman willing to sell him her body for a few American coins?

His broad shoulders seemed too wide for his thin frame. The expression on his young face told her, as it always did, that he, too, was carrying a weight. There was a hint of defeat in his walk, but she sensed strength and purpose in him as well.

His gaze startled her. Their eyes met, then Sook Hee's eyes quickly lowered. She had no desire to appear forward. By the time she lifted her gaze, he had disappeared behind her neighbor's house.

She silently edged closer to the road and peered around the corner of the house.

"Oh!" she gasped. He had stopped in the road, looking back in her direction. Again their eyes met, and she pulled back quickly, embarrassed, retreating to the safety and anonymity of the water barrel.

She couldn't believe that she had given in to the temptation of taking notice of this man. There was nothing immoral or sinister in her heart, but he *was* tall and handsome, and she was intrigued that he seemed so different from the men who made advances as she was leaving work each day.

She dipped the wooden ladle into the icy water barrel, her heart pounding, trying to ignore the inquisitive eyes of the soldier, now standing just on the other side of the rough wooden fence separating her home from the dirt road. She was embarrassed now, and uneasy, that her casual curiosity had resulted in this face-to-face encounter with a man she did not know. And yet … Sook Hee surprised herself. Using the little English she had learned from the Americans at the base over the last few months and with a slight bow, head lowered and eyes focused on the ground, she softly said, "I make tea. You like?"

CHAPTER 3

A Bit of Warmth

The young American soldier ducked as he followed the girl through the wooden doorway into a dark, chilled room. She opened a window shutter, and the late-afternoon sunshine pushed back the shadows. Despite all the signs of poverty, the room was clean, earthy, and homey. In the small living space was a *soban*, a short-legged table, and a *yo*, or bedroll, arranged neatly in the corner.

The girl stirred the coals in the potbellied stove, which soon blazed into a meager fire, providing a bit of warmth. As she quietly brewed the tea, the young man looked around, his thoughts swirling. *How can she survive on so little? She seems so vulnerable and innocent compared to most of the other young women I've seen. How did she end up here, in this village, apparently alone?*

As soon as she had spoken to him, even though she had still been looking down, he had recognized her as the quiet, pretty woman who worked in the base mess hall. Oddly, though, he had not recognized her voice—in fact, he believed that this was the first time he had heard her voice, even though he saw her a few times a week. But there was something distinctive—and lovely—in the way she held her head, in the shape of her jaw and her cheekbone. The tea steeped, and the sweet aroma filled the room. There wasn't much conversation, since his Korean was even less than the few English words the girl spoke. Sook Hee, she said her name was. He watched her delicate hands preparing the tea; her grace and her simple beauty touched his deep-seated loneliness. She was elegant—she could have been a princess: quiet, simple, and beautiful. She was timid yet seemed pleased to have him as a guest in her home. He felt the stress and anguish in his hardened soul begin to melt away.

He had come into this cold, hard war a typical American boy, but the stench of death and the horrific images that had been seared indelibly into his senses had turned him into a man. He had seen much … and had changed much. He worried about returning to a family that probably wouldn't understand the man he had become. Even so, he ached for them, so far away, and wished he was with them on this Christmas Day.

As Sook Hee gently placed his cup of tea on the table, her hand brushed his. She quickly looked up and searched his eyes. Her warm touch alerted his senses. He stared back. Her gaze softened. He sensed that she recognized the anguish in his heart. He was overcome first with gratitude—then with longing.

The young American knew better. A girlfriend waited for him at home. His parents had taught him that intimacy was sacred and should be reserved for marriage.

They gave themselves to each other.

CHAPTER 4

Alone

One day as Sook Hee worked in the cafeteria, she leaned over the slop bin to scrape the remains of a meal off a soiled plate. Her stomach tightened with aching nausea that would not relent. Reluctantly, she admitted to herself why she felt so sick.

She had feared for weeks now that she carried the child of the American soldier. Now she was sure.

But he was gone. He had spoken to her one day a few weeks before, as she left the base at the end of her workday. She did not understand English well enough to understand everything he said, but she recognized some words: "Leave … America … home … good-bye."

"Oh … then please … have good life," she had replied, struggling for the right words. She had suspected at that time she was pregnant, but what good would it do to tell him?

He reached for her hand and stared into her eyes. She sensed that he cared, that he was a kind man, but she could not meet his gaze and quickly turned away.

"You ... good life too," she understood him to say as she walked swiftly toward home.

Sook Hee could not move down the alley fast enough that evening. Her world was spinning out of control. Her situation felt so impossible that she wasn't certain she could go on living. She collapsed on the floor of her small, dark room. Sobs of anguish filled the dark stillness.

"What will I do? I don't know! I don't know!" she repeated softly, rocking back and forth, arms wrapped around her legs.

⁕

Five months later, Sook Hee was struggling to hide her growing belly under a loose dress. Shame and worry had become her constant companions. She would surely soon lose her job and needed help. She really had only one choice if she was to go on living: She needed to face her extended family.

Sook Hee had put off that journey, a day's walk, as long as she could. But the month of May was a good time to travel. The winter had thawed, the sun's warmth was gentle, and the humidity of summer had not yet set in. She abandoned her stark room in the village and headed toward the exposure of her shame.

She walked slowly, taking in what springtime beauty remained—the countryside had been cleared of nearly all foliage by war and poverty. Even so, wildflowers had sprung up along the path. Sook Hee plucked one and tucked it behind her ear, knowing that her long, jet-black hair would make the white blossom glisten. Not quite ready to face her family, she lingered beside a quiet stream to soak her tired, swollen feet and eat her lunch of barley wrapped in seaweed.

The gray of dusk had fallen by the time Sook Hee reached her ancestral home, where her eldest uncle, his wife, and their children lived with her grandparents. She stood in front of the heavy, wooden gate with iron handles that guarded the one-story, mud-walled, thatched-roof house. Sighing deeply, she pushed it open and shuffled quietly through the barren courtyard until she reached the steps leading to the porch. Lantern light from inside shone through the rice-paper interior wall and dotted its surface. She could hear the low rumbling of voices and scraping of metal chopsticks.

Hesitating at the lowest step, Sook Hee tilted her chin and called out, "Hello. I am here. This is Sook Hee."

There was a pause, movement. The rice-paper door slid open.

"Sook Hee?" Her grandmother rushed onto the terrace. "Sook Hee! Sook Hee!"

Grandmother hurried down to where Sook Hee stood. Before Sook Hee could reply, her overjoyed grandmother grabbed her hands, vigorously shaking them up and down, splashes of light reflecting in her upturned crinkled eyes. The rest of the family, some pleased, some curious, gathered in the doorway and on the porch.

It happened so fast. With a final enthusiastic downward pump, the older woman's hand struck the soft curve of Sook Hee's growing belly. Her expression froze. The lantern light had spilled out of the room and spread across

Sook Hee's delicate frame. The shameful truth registered on each of their faces. Her family's silent stares magnified the shame Sook Hee already knew.

"Come, young lady," her grandmother said.

Trembling, Sook Hee climbed the porch stairs and entered the home, unable to meet the eyes of her relatives.

Grandmother snapped to her daughter-in-law, "Jae Hwa, take the children to bed."

Once the children were out of the room, the questions flew faster than Sook Hee could respond.

"What have you done?" her uncle bellowed. "Who is the father?"

"How can you now marry honorably?" asked Grandmother.

"How will we take away this shame?" Grandfather cried, his face twisted with emotion.

Overwhelmed and faint with hunger, Sook Hee remained quiet. There was, after all, little she could say in her own defense. The sliding door wasn't completely closed. She stared back over her shoulder through the crack into the fallen darkness. Was it too late to go back? "Perhaps I shouldn't have come," she said so softly her words could not be heard.

The sudden force of her uncle's hand across her face sent her staggering backward, and she collapsed onto the floor of the house. Closing her eyes tightly, she stayed on the floor. She was not surprised; this was what she'd expected.

"You've brought dishonor to our family," her uncle said

coldly. "You are a disgrace to us and to your ancestors! This child may never have our name."

His words settled deep into her soul.

As Sook Hee pushed herself up, cheek stinging, her family members walked out the door, leaving her alone with her thoughts. As bad as that had been, there was even worse to come—her family did not yet know that the baby she carried had a white father. In Korea, having a fatherless child of mixed blood brought impurities to the ancestral bloodlines. It was culturally unacceptable—a disgrace. And children who were not given a family name literally had no birthright and lived unacknowledged. They were rejected. Worthless. Nothings.

Sook Hee regretted her time of weakness with the young American soldier. Because of it, her future would be forever different than it would have been. Sook Hee clutched her stomach and wept. She feared what lay ahead—not only for herself, but even more so for her unborn child, this life growing inside her.

Despite the shame she had brought upon her family, Sook Hee was still a part of them. She carried her father's name and was the daughter of her uncle's brother. She knew she would be allowed to remain. Family honor would keep her safe from prying eyes and gossip.

At least she was no longer alone.

CHAPTER 5

Destiny's Child

Yoon Myoung—*Destiny*—was born on September 25, 1954, a beautiful and healthy baby girl. The soft crease in her upper eyelids and her gentle waves of light brown hair set her apart from her relatives.

As time passed, it became more difficult to keep this child from the suspicious gaze of others. Neighbors and those in the village began to talk quietly among themselves.

"Have you seen Sook Hee's child?" a woman gathering water from the village well asked those gathered around.

"It's a disgrace to her family," said another. "She must have been with a foreigner when she lived in the city."

"The Kim family will never accept Sook Hee into their family now," whispered another. "She is betrothed to their son, but they will not have a mixed-blood child in their midst."

The Korean people had suffered greatly during the Japanese occupation before WWII. Then the communist occupation had come, and then the Korean War—their cultural identity had been ripped away. Although grateful to their Western liberators, their greatest desire was to rebuild their lives, reclaim their land, and forget their pain. The sight of mixed-blood children such as Yoon Myoung stirred up their anger, frustration, and hurt. The foreigners may have fought to preserve South Korea's independence, but they were not permitted into Korean families, heritages, or bloodlines. Little Yoon Myoung had been born into a nation that was repelled by her and had no room for her.

⊷⊶

In the five years after the cease-fire, the adult villagers worked hard to recover their land. Most were too busy to take notice of Sook Hee and her little girl, and the others purposely ignored them.

One day Yoon Myoung, now an active and observant four-year-old, sat on the wooden floor of the wraparound porch at the front of the house. The planks had been smoothed by a century of use.

The activities of her family in the courtyard before her captured her attention. While her great-grandfather and uncle played *baduk*, her mama and auntie hung laundry, attaching each piece of clothing with care to the rope strung between two wooden poles. Great-Grandmother was grinding sesame seed in the large stone bowl with a smooth stone. Her cousins' occasional shrieks of discovery while playing hide-and-seek echoed off the courtyard walls.

This house was a shrine to the ancestors of Sook Hee, who had lived and died here forever. Yoon Myoung's knowledge of such things was only beginning to develop and grow.

She was tiny and beautiful in a way that was both Western and Asian. Her eyes were a bit rounder than the other children from this house and village. Her hair, lighter in color than the rest, had a soft curl to it. She was Korean, but there were hints of something else, like a shadowy mist. Though it was difficult to pinpoint, everyone saw it.

Yoon Myoung knew she was different from the way the adults looked at her, the way they spoke to her. But this was not true of the children in the village and her cousins, who simply enjoyed playing, and she loved it just as much. It was with the children that she felt most free.

She tried to make sense of the behavior of the adults. "Mama," she said, as her mother went about her duties. "Why are some of the other mommies mean to me?"

Her mama stopped what she was doing and sat down next to her. "Tell me what you mean, Yoon Myoung."

"They yell at me to get away from the other children," she said. "Sometimes they push me out of the way. But I don't do anything wrong!"

Pulling Yoon Myoung close, her mama said, "Yoon Myoung, sometimes people can be cruel. They aren't even aware of what they do."

"But Great-Grandfather never talks to me either." She watched her great-grandfather, distracted by the game of hide-and-seek going on around him, taking a moment to smile quietly at his grandchildren, patting their heads as they ran by.

Her cousins were loved, nurtured, and cherished, Yoon

Myoung could see. But she was often ignored. Despite the innocent trust of childhood, she felt the subtle differences.

"Yoon Myoung, I love you, and I think you are special. That's what matters," smiled Sook Hee.

This reassurance from her mama, along with the routines of family life, comforted Yoon Myoung. She returned her mama's smile as Sook Hee rose and returned to her laundry.

Yoon Myoung stared beyond where her mother and aunt worked to the brown straw-and-mud-stucco wall. If she walked past the wooden, black-handled gate, she knew she would be on the village dirt road, which turned to mire when the rains came. The size of Yoon Myoung's world was limited to this home and this village. Despite being different, she had bloomed in its security and warmth.

The grinding of stone on sesame seeds continued, bringing an assurance of food for tomorrow.

She glanced above at the overhanging gray-thatched roof, where a pair of birds were building a nest, swooping in and out. "Hello, birdies," she called. Both birds flew off, and although she felt disappointed, she knew they would return with a piece of grass in their beaks. When they did, a few moments later, she called with joy, "Mama, they came back!"

As the orange sun set below the horizon, the women's chatter gradually moved inside the house. Yoon Myoung followed her mama. Their home had three rooms opening south onto the wooden porch. In typical Korean style, the wooden floors were raised so that they did not touch the ground. This helped to moderate the heat and humidity of the summer months. Stones covered with mud, placed under the raised floor and heated twice each day, provided plenty of warmth in the winter months. The kitchen, three feet lower than the main house, was connected to the east end where it was sheltered from the sun.

After the evening meal, one by one the children crawled into the warmth of their bedrolls. Sook Hee drew the rice-paper doors, isolating her and Yoon Myoung from the rest of the family, and brought out some worn blankets to place on the honey-colored, wax-papered floor.

Resting her head in her mama's lap, Yoon Myoung looked up and saw tenderness in her mother's eyes, as she always did. Cuddled in her nest on the floor, Yoon Myoung felt loved, nurtured, and protected. Lulled by the hushed voices of the preoccupied adults in the next room and the delicate stroking of her hair by her mother, Yoon Myoung drifted off to sleep.

CHAPTER 6

"Are You Ever Afraid?"

One morning Yoon Myoung and Sook Hee were alone in the house. Climbing into her lap, the child looked into her mama's face. Sook Hee was so lovely, but her eyes always seemed sad.

"Little girl, are you happy?" Sook Hee asked.

Yoon Myoung loved these moments sitting with her mama. "Yes, Mommy."

"What makes you happy?" questioned Sook Hee.

"Yesterday I rode on the front bars of a bicycle for the first time," the little girl grinned. "The wind blew in my face. It was much more fun than sitting on the back of the bicycle."

"What else makes you happy?" continued Sook Hee.

Yoon Myoung paused, twirling her hair in her fingers. "Uncle put me on his shoulders in the village and galloped around like a horse. That made me giggle!"

"Is there more that makes you happy?"

"Mommy, why are you asking me so many questions?"

Sook Hee only looked into her daughter's eyes.

Yoon Myoung continued, "Remember when I was a baby, you would tie me on your back when you walked in the village and when you worked in the rice paddies? I liked that a lot. I like it when you hold me."

Sook Hee pulled her daughter close against her rough tunic. Yoon Myoung wished the moment would last forever.

"Tell me more," Sook Hee said.

"I like lying in my blankets at night listening to your voice on the other side of the wall." She paused. "Oh—and do you remember, Mama, the day we went to the village, and I swung on the swing that hung from the old tree? That was so much fun!" Yoon Myoung squirmed with excitement, remembering. "You stood by the old stone wall and watched me."

⇥⇤

Yes, Sook Hee remembered that day. But what Yoon Myoung did not know is that while Sook Hee stood by the wall watching her daughter, she had also overheard the whispers of the villagers.

"I don't like that little *tougee* around here," one murmured.

"She will never have a name, that mixed-blood, bastard child!" another added.

Caressing her daughter's face as Yoon Myoung snuggled in her lap, Sook Hee tried hard to hide, as she always did, the inward battle that had raged within her every day since Yoon Myoung's birth: Understanding her culture and heritage, yet loving this child others called a *tougee*, a child of mixed blood, a child with no father, a child of nothing.

She asked her daughter another question, a question she had not intended to ask. "Are you ever afraid?"

"Um … one time I was very scared, but I don't know why." Yoon Myoung's voice became quieter. "I can't remember what happened, but I hid during the day in the blanket closet for a long time because something made me very afraid. Auntie found me and scolded me for being in the closet."

Her daughter paused, then continued. "Do you remember when I came home from the village with blood running down my face? I was so scared that day. I was scared you would get mad at me for getting blood on my dress. Can you still see the scar, Mama?"

Sook Hee's finger shook as she traced the scar across her daughter's forehead. She watched Yoon Myoung's trusting face relax into joy at her touch.

CHAPTER 7

The Long Walk

Time moved on. The days unfolded like the bedroll Sook Hee opened every evening for Yoon Myoung. It had been used by ancestors Yoon Myoung had never known. The blankets, like Yoon Myoung's ancestors, had survived the hardships of war and of time.

One night, Yoon Myoung crawled under her covering and lay in her bed thinking about the festive day that had just ended. What a day it had been! It was the time of *Chuseok*, the fifteenth day of the eighth lunar month. Sook Hee had dressed Yoon Myoung that morning in a multicolored Korean *jeogori* and *hanbok* that had been sewn for this annual event. She had been taken to her great-grandparents' room where, on her knees, she had bowed repeatedly to them. As the patriarch and matriarch, her great-grandparents were given great honor by the rest of the family.

Together, the entire family had practiced *bulcho*, the tradition of cutting the weeds from around the ancestral burial place of their family. Then they had gathered around the household shrines to offer respects to their ancestors.

They watched the village children swinging, playing *nol-ttwigi*—a type of standing seesaw—and flying rice-paper kites. The adzuki beans, chestnuts, jujube fruit, and new crop grains delighted Yoon Myoung, whose daily meals on normal days consisted only of rice, barley, and *kimchee*. She relished the sweet *songpyeon* rice cakes, prepared only for festival days.

With warm memories of the day floating through her mind, Yoon Myoung drifted off to sleep.

She awoke abruptly during the dark night to voices in the next room growing louder and louder. The shouts echoed throughout the house as each person's words jumped on top of the other's. Yoon Myoung was confused. What could be wrong?

Cuddled in her blankets, she could hear the quivering voice of her mama. Why was she crying? Listening to her mother gasp for air between sobs, Yoon Myoung knew something had to be terribly wrong!

"Mommy, why are you crying?" she said out loud, although no one listened. Yoon Myoung dug deeper into her coverings, seeking comfort.

She could make out her great-uncle's voice. "There is no choice, Sook Hee! You can't stay here forever. The husband we have found for you will not take you with this child." On that final word, the thud of his fist pounding the table caused Yoon Myoung to jump.

"It is time!" scolded her great-aunt. "You and the girl cannot stay here any longer!"

Yoon Myoung heard her mother weeping. *What girl?* she wondered. *Are they talking about me?*

She heard her mother's choking words, but they were too soft to make out. She easily heard Uncle's shouted reply. "You should have thought about those things five years ago! He will not accept you as his wife with a fatherless, foreign mixed-blood. If you want to be taken care of and want this man to marry you, the little girl must leave."

"Please, no!" her mother cried. "She is my daughter. She is family!"

"She is not *our* family. She has no father," hissed her great-uncle. "The tougee must leave our home and our village. If she stays anywhere near here, she will be the shame of your husband, your ancestors, and us. Your life is over if you keep her here. She must leave!"

"Don't call her that!" Sook Hee pled. "She is my daughter!"

Tougee. Yoon Myoung had heard that word before. She had noticed that her mama always became silent whenever anyone called Yoon Myoung by that name. Although she didn't understand what it meant, she was sure it wasn't good.

The vibration made by her mother's bare feet running along the wooden porch increased as the rice-paper door to her room suddenly slid open.

Yoon Myoung whispered, "What's wrong, Mommy?"

Sook Hee knelt beside Yoon Myoung, her eyes swollen with tears.

Yoon Myoung said again, "Mommy, what is wrong?"

Her mama quietly wept as she swept Yoon Myoung into her arms. "Don't be afraid, my daughter. It will work out."

Yoon Myoung relaxed as her mother rocked her, and

her eyes again grew heavy. She fell asleep in her mother's arms.

Morning dawned with the crowing of a rooster. Yoon Myoung crawled out from beneath the bedding, folded the blankets, and placed them in the closet. Sook Hee came into the room with a small cloth bag and welcomed the little girl to a new day. A smile and a hand on her head didn't hide the sadness Yoon Myoung saw in her mother's pinched expression. She remembered the events of the night before.

"Mama … I think I had a nightmare last night," Yoon Myoung said.

Sook Hee put a slender finger in front of her lips. "My precious girl, everything will be all right." She hesitated, then said, "We are going on a long, pleasant walk."

A special treat! An outdoor adventure with her mother! "Mommy, may I wear my new, striped *jeogori*?" she asked, forgetting about her "dream."

"No, Yoon Myoung, put on your hemp *hanbok*."

"But isn't today special, like yesterday?"

Sook Hee shook her head.

Excited nonetheless, Yoon Myoung swiftly changed into her everyday clothes.

※

Yoon Myoung was eager to begin their adventure, but Sook Hee hesitated on the front porch. Yoon Myoung waited impatiently, looking at her mother, and then tugged her hand gently. "Mama?" she said, but her mother continued to gaze at the sky and treetops above the fence, and then she placed her hand on Yoon Myoung's head and began to sing softly one of the old familiar songs. Yoon Myoung was always comforted by her mama's songs. But what was happening? Why were they stopping?

Still looking up at her mother, Yoon Myoung asked, "Is someone going to come with us?"

Sook Hee shook her head and stepped slowly down to the dirt courtyard. Yoon Myoung followed. She slipped her fingers into her mother's slim but calloused hand. They walked past the grinding bowl and the clothesline, and Sook Hee took hold of the large, iron ring to pull open the gate. As they stepped over the elevated threshold onto the dirt road, Yoon Myoung glanced back and wondered why her uncle, her aunt, and her cousins watched from the porch—and why they looked so solemn. She waved to them, but only her cousins returned the gesture.

The morning air was crisp, but the day's sunshine was already warming Yoon Myoung's cheeks. The village lane gradually turned into a long, straight road newly lined with birch saplings. Yoon Myoung looked up eagerly as the trees whistled in the wind, and the leaves sounded like the clapping of hands.

"Mommy, I don't see any birds. Are they up there today?" she asked.

There was no response from her mother, so Yoon Myoung said, "Mommy, did you hear me? I don't see any birds. Are they up there?"

"Oh yes, precious. The birds will always be there."

They walked on for quite some time. Today felt like an

adventure. They walked beyond the village gathering place to other places Yoon Myoung had never been.

The sun was not yet overhead when Yoon Myoung heard an unfamiliar sound in the distance and asked, "Mommy, what's that *whoo, whoo* sound?"

Pointing to a large brick building in the distance, Sook Hee said, "We are going to where the noise is coming from."

As they neared, Sook Hee helped Yoon Myoung dodge ox carts and bicyclists weaving around one another. Scrap-metal buses spewed black smoke, causing Yoon Myoung to sneeze. She couldn't take her eyes off one peasant who had balanced layers of eggs between his handle bars, had loaded wares on his head, and was steadying a wiggly pig tied onto the back of his seat.

Still trying to take in all of the commotion around her, Yoon Myoung watched her mother walk up to a small window and slide some money across the counter to a man. He gave her a small piece of paper in return and pointed to a bench on the large open platform behind him. Yoon Myoung thought maybe her mother was buying some food for a treat. Sook Hee took her hand and led her to the bench, where they sat side by side.

"Are we getting some food, Mommy?" Yoon Myoung asked.

"No, I brought along some food for the day," replied her mama.

Yoon Myoung noticed two long, shiny iron rails on the ground with thick brown pieces of wood between them. It seemed like they stretched to the mountains in one direction and into the rice paddies in the other. She wondered what these were for. On the horizon, Yoon Myoung caught sight of something black belching smoke into the brilliant blue sky. The sound it made—the same *whoo, whoo* noise Yoon Myoung had heard earlier—caused Sook Hee to stand up. Soon a large black dragon rolled toward them on top of the rails. The rumbling became louder as the black thing came closer, and Yoon Myoung wasn't sure whether she should be scared or excited. She held her mommy's hand tighter.

Yoon Myoung had never seen anything like this before. Coughing up smoke, the huge noisy thing stopped at the platform where they were standing. Yoon Myoung was startled to see people coming out of the doors of big boxes connected to the black dragon. Warm steam came from underneath it and swirled around Yoon Myoung and Sook Hee. It reminded her of the fog drifting over the rice paddies that morning as they came down from the mountains. It was magic to watch people disappear into the steam cloud and reappear in another place.

The people tumbling out, most of them struggling with crates or cloth bundles strapped to their backs or tied on top of their heads, were excitedly greeted by bowing relatives. Hoping they were going to ride in one of these boxes, Yoon Myoung began to bounce with glee.

"Mama, what is this—a dragon?" Yoon Myoung asked.

Sook Hee was not smiling. She turned to Yoon Myoung and said, "No, Yoon Myoung, this is not a dragon. It's called a train."

Yoon Myoung bounced up and down on her tiptoes.

"A train? A train, Mommy? Are we going to take a ride on the train?"

Sook Hee took Yoon Myoung's hand and climbed up into the passenger car. She hesitated at the top of the steps as if not sure what to do, then turned toward the back of the train. At the nearest open window seat, Sook Hee gently settled her daughter onto the worn wooden bench. She drew out the little cloth bag and placed it on the overhead shelf above Yoon Myoung. Crouching, Sook Hee took her daughter's rounded fingers in her hands.

Yoon Myoung looked up at her mother and saw tears on Sook Hee's cheeks. "What's wrong, Mama? Is the smoke getting in your eyes?"

Sook Hee's voice shook as she said, "You're going to take a train ride." She spoke the strange-sounding name of another village. "When you get off, your uncle will meet you and take care of you."

"You're coming with me, Mommy—aren't you?" Yoon Myoung had never been separated from her mama. She felt her muscles tighten and her head spin. Why would her mama put her on this train by herself? How would she find her way?

Sook Hee said, "You must go alone. You must go to your uncle, and he will take care of you. There is plenty of food for the day in this sack."

Yoon Myoung said, "And then you'll come for me, Mommy?"

Sook Hee rose. "Yes, I will. Be a good and brave girl."

Yoon Myoung squeezed her mama's hands tightly and did not want to let go, but her mama gently pulled her hands free. Yoon Myoung watched Sook Hee turn and walk away.

"Mommy told me it would be all right," she whispered. It *would* be all right. She was going to an uncle's home, and she would see her mommy again soon.

So why did her heart feel like it was cracking? Her heart had never felt like this before.

Yoon Myoung looked out the window and saw her mama standing on the platform. She leaned out and cried, "You're coming for me soon?"

Sook Hee's cheeks were covered in tears. She did not speak, but slowly waved back with a handkerchief in her hand. The locomotive's whistle blew, and the train started to move. Steam rolled out from under its belly and billowed around Sook Hee. Yoon Myoung waved to her as she grew smaller and more distant. Sook Hee waved back, until she was swallowed by the steam and disappeared.

PART 2

CHAPTER 8

The Train Station

The bench facing Yoon Myoung was occupied by an old man who looked like her great-grandfather. He nodded off to sleep while the two young women seated next to him conversed rapidly. Sitting next to Yoon Myoung, a middle-aged man read a tattered newspaper and occasionally glanced her way. The swaying of the train soothed Yoon Myoung; it was like being rocked. Ignored by her bench companions, she held her cloth sack of food on her lap and sang softly in time to the clickety-clack of the train wheels. She amused herself by occasionally sticking her head out the window. She enjoyed feeling the wind against her cheeks and the force of her hair flying behind her. Yoon Myoung had never gone this fast before. Bicycle rides were exciting, but nothing compared to this!

It will be all right—she reminded herself of her mama's parting words. She was going to see new relatives, and her mama would come soon.

The train traveled on for what seemed like a long time. When the whistle blew and the train started slowing down, wheels screeching, Yoon Myoung peered out the window and saw a platform that looked much like the one where she had left her mama. Her seatmates stood, gathered their belongings, and disembarked with their bundles. Yoon Myoung climbed onto the wooden bench, stretched as high as she could reach to grab her little cloth bag, and followed the people out of the train car.

Standing on the platform, Yoon Myoung observed the uniting of family and friends. She watched as a mother and her children welcomed a man home with lively bows. Yoon Myoung was captivated by their happiness. Her mama had said her uncle would be here to meet her, and she hoped that he would be pleased to see her. She would perform many deep bows.

She examined the faces of the men on the platform, seeking a man who was searching for her. In their excitement, men and women bumped into her. Other people came and disappeared into the train.

Suddenly the platform was empty. The train that had carried her here began to huff and puff; the wheels started to turn. The whistle screamed, and once again the train was moving. Steam enveloped her.

Afraid to move for fear of missing her uncle, Yoon Myoung stood attentively and waited. The shadows grew longer; the sky slowly darkened.

A uniformed man briskly emerged from the ticket office onto the empty platform. He squinted down at Yoon Myoung over his round eyeglasses. "Tougee, why are you still here?" he snapped. "You must go on!"

There was that word again … the word that made her feel uncomfortable inside.

"Are you my uncle?" Yoon Myoung asked. "I'm waiting for my uncle."

"*Your uncle?* No, I'm not your uncle." He tilted his head and looked at her. "What does he look like?"

"I don't know, but my mommy told me I must wait for him here."

"Well, it's getting dark. I don't think anyone is coming for you, tougee."

Young Myoung felt a rush of panic. Her mother had told her that her uncle would meet her at the station. She *had* to do what her mother said to do! "I must wait *here* for my uncle!" Yoon Myoung said, nearly in tears, her voice rising.

The stationmaster looked at her sadly. "No one is coming for you," he said, his voice quieter than before. "Now go on! We need to close down for the night." With that, he gave her a gentle push.

Yoon Myoung's breaths came quickly. Her heart pounded against her chest as she moved away from the now-dark, empty train station. She had never felt like this before. Stepping out into the street, she tried to decide what to do, where to go. She needed her mama to tell her. Yoon Myoung's body was shaking, and she didn't know how to stop it.

An overturned ox cart leaned against the wall of the station. Peering underneath it, Yoon Myoung thought, *I'll wait here, and in the morning my uncle will come to get me.*

Maybe her body would stop shaking if she could sit down. She crawled under the cart and scooted on top of some old hay, as close to the wall as she could. She clutched her cloth bag to her chest. She could breathe better here beneath the ox cart, hidden from the street. She felt protected.

She felt lumps inside the cloth bag. What had her mama given her? Yoon Myoung opened it. Barley, pickles, spinach wrapped in seaweed, and even a boiled egg!

Hungry, she ate all of it, but the comfort the food provided disappeared quickly. Yoon Myoung heard dogs barking in the distance. She began to imagine someone reaching in and grabbing her ankles. Her heart began to pound again, and her body shook. Tucking her legs against her chest, she put the cloth over her head and rocked back and forth.

"It will be all right … it will be all right … it will be all right," she repeated in a whisper, eventually dropping into an exhausted sleep.

During the night, Yoon Myoung was awakened by the howling of a dog. Her heart raced. For a moment, she didn't know where she was. She grabbed for her warm blankets, but the hay she slept on scratched her cheek and shocked her back to reality.

"Uncle will come for me tomorrow," she whispered. "And Mama will come soon, Mama will come soon. It will be all right." Soothing herself, she curled up again into a tight ball and fell back to sleep.

⁘

Dawn came, and with it all the noises of a town readying for another day. The clatter of feet on the platform and the whistle of the early morning train roused Yoon Myoung. She awakened and remembered. There were bells in the distance, ox carts rumbling on the gravel road, and the calls of people preparing for work.

Today she would meet her uncle.

She barely noticed her growling tummy as she scrambled out from under the ox cart. Pausing to brush the dried bits of straw off her clothing and pat down her hair, Yoon Myoung darted back into the train station and positioned herself on the platform near the ticket booth. People came, people went. No one looked at her with recognition. The minutes ticked by. Hours passed.

Mommy told me to wait, so I must wait here, she reminded herself.

She was determined to find her uncle today. Occasionally, she felt the stare of the stationmaster, but when she returned his gaze, he quickly busied himself with a passenger or looked to the ground. Although she was eager to talk to someone, Yoon Myoung was relieved that he didn't approach her.

But at the very end of the day, he stepped onto the platform and said, "Tougee, no one is coming for you. You must leave."

"My mama said that I must wait for my uncle. I must wait right here!"

He drew in a slow breath through his nose and forced it out. His lips tightened, his jaw clenched, and he prodded her shoulder with his finger. "You cannot wait here. Do you hear me? No one is coming for you!"

Hanging her head in confusion and alarm, Yoon Myoung obeyed. The thumping in her chest started again. Tears burned her eyes as she stumbled back to the ox cart.

Hungry and alone for a second night, thoughts raced through her head. *Mommy told me my uncle would be here to meet me. How am I going to find him? Mommy, I need you! You said you would come for me!*

Yoon Myoung sat quietly under her ox cart for a long time, thinking, as the evening sun set and darkness engulfed her yet again. *The man in the uniform is right*, she thought. *No one is coming for me! I don't know what to do!*

Her body shook with the distress of being alone and her dread of being on her own. What would she eat? She was already starving! Where would she sleep? Who would protect her from dogs, from mean people? Who would tell her stories and make her laugh? How could she get home to her mama? Yoon Myoung began to cry softly. Her whimpers soon turned to uncontrollable sobs. She realized that she would need to leave this ox cart, her only safe place in this strange village, and the thought terrified her.

A plan began to push to the surface of her churning thoughts.

The black train brought me here. Tomorrow morning, if I walk on the tracks back in the direction I came from, the iron rails will take me back to where I left my mama. From there I can find the pretty tree-lined road. I will keep walking until I find the big wooden gate with the black rings opening to my home.

With this new plan, her fears began to dissipate. And as her fears eased, she was suddenly overcome by gnawing hunger. But there was nothing left to eat.

She repeated again, "It will be all right. It will be all right. I will find my way back home ... I will get back to my mama ... " She drifted off to a fitful sleep.

CHAPTER 9

Tougee

The autumn morning sun gently awakened Yoon Myoung. She crawled out from under the ox cart and stood facing the sunlight. She raised her arms above her head and stretched. Bits of hay from her makeshift bed fell around her from her arms and hair, and she shook herself to dislodge them, then carefully picked off those that remained. She knelt beside the cart, thrust her hand back into the smelly straw, and retrieved her cloth food sack. Its emptiness magnified her hunger pains. She fingered it and had a sudden memory of her mama tying a cloth around her head when she worked in the rice paddies. Yoon Myoung spread the bag open, placed it on her head, and tied its corners in small knots to cinch it down. Pleased with the results, she turned with determination and climbed the wooden steps to the train platform one last time to look into the faces of the men gathered there. She tried to ignore the station manager's glares—and he was the only one to notice her. After a few hours, Yoon Myoung gave in to his scowls and abandoned the train station.

She scrambled off the platform and made her way around the train station to the empty tracks, where she balanced on the first rail with her left foot. Counting five steps across the tie, she hopped onto the other rail and balanced herself for as long as she could. Then she jumped into the tall grass next to the empty tracks and intently looked first to the right, then left. She knew that she had come from the left. Finally, full of anticipation, her heart beating faster, she turned east into the sunshine, toward her mama. She began to walk through the tall grass.

The day was hot, and after only a few minutes, her skin felt sweaty and scratchy. A few minutes more, and the sun was scorching her body, except for what was covered by her dress and the cloth on her head. The grass beside the train tracks was tall and soft, hard to move through, so Yoon Myoung moved up onto the tracks themselves and entertained herself by scampering between the rails and the ties. But soon the game lost its appeal. Her short, skinny legs couldn't quite stretch from one wooden tie to the next. The attempt made her legs sore and made her sweat even more. She tried balancing each step on top of the iron rail, but it took too much concentration. Besides, the metal rails were scorching!

She walked along for what seemed like forever. And the longer she walked, the more her little legs ached and the hungrier and thirstier she felt. But when she caught sight of a village in the distance, energy surged through her. She set off running as fast as her legs could carry her. This must be home! She would find her mama!

"Mama! Mama! Here I am!" she yelled.

The mud-walled, tiled- and thatched-roof houses looked so much like her village. But as she rushed past a stone wall and then past the first house, she slowed down and stopped. This was not her village! These villagers stared at her, making her feel ugly. No one looked familiar.

Yoon Myoung felt a deep ache for her mama. She longed to be wrapped in her mama's arms. When Mama was near, everything was better. Tears of disappointment stung her eyes, and she turned back toward the tracks.

Just before she reached them, she spotted a man and a small boy walking toward the village. Yoon Myoung was nervous, but she was also painfully hungry. She approached them. "Uncle?" she said, bowing. "I am so hungry. Do you have something that I could eat?"

The man pulled the little boy away from her.

"We have nothing for tougees," he barked.

Tears pooled in her eyes, and she drew closer. "But why? Why can't you share? I'm hungry."

The man shoved her away and turned his back.

"Please. I'm so hungry. Don't you have anything for me to eat?" she persisted.

Ignoring her, the man tightened his grip on the boy and quickened his pace.

⁑

Her growling and empty stomach would not let Yoon Myoung forget that it had been two days since she had devoured the contents of the cloth sack her mama had sent with her. First she trudged along the tracks, then tunneled through the tall, willowy grasses on the embankment above the rice fields. She remembered that her mama sometimes pulled stalks from the ground and let her snack on the white parts of the root. Yoon Myoung grabbed a handful of plants and tugged until the earth reluctantly released the shoots. She washed the bulbs in a murky irrigation ditch and began to nibble. They were watery and had a nutty taste. Yoon Myoung sucked and chewed on them until her tummy began to cramp.

With renewed energy, she scrambled back up to the tracks. It was beginning to get dark. She had passed only one village on this first day, and it hadn't been hers. The faces of the many who had scorned her the past few days began to play across her mind. She shuddered.

"Why is everyone so mean to me? I want my mama!"

Too tired to walk any farther, Yoon Myoung slid back down to the grassy bottom of the dry gully to find a place to sleep. With her white, rubber, canoe-shaped *gomushins*, she stomped the grass flat and made a bed for the night. Removing the lunch cloth and smoothing it over her chest, Yoon Myoung lay on her side, placed her hands behind her head protectively, and curled her legs up close to her body. She turned her head and looked up past her elbow at the stars. She thought immediately of the comforts of home, and tears burned down her cheeks.

When will I see Mama again? Why won't anyone help me? I'm so scared.

Her body ached, and her stomach had felt uneasy since eating the green shoots—and she was still hungry. Her mama must be looking for her. She wanted to hear her mama's voice singing softly; that always made her feel better. *Why did you send me away, Mama? Why couldn't I stay with you? Why didn't I jump from the train and run back to you?*

She curled tighter, into a ball, trying to keep her gaze on the stars. But almost immediately she fell asleep.

≫≪

The next day, as Yoon Myoung walked through the tall grass along the rail bed, she saw several children ahead on the tracks. Who could they be? She wasn't close to a village. She stopped, lay down on her tummy at the edge of the grass, and watched from a distance.

An older boy searched for something beside the tracks, and finally stooped with a cry and picked up a gadget. The other children gathered around him, all looking at the item he held in his hand. Yoon Myoung watched, squinting, as he carefully placed the object on the metal rail. The rest of the children stretched out on their bellies, and each pressed an ear to the rail. They waited.

Finally, one of the boys shouted, "It's coming, it's coming!" and the children jumped up and ran into the grass alongside the tracks.

Yoon Myoung first saw the black smoke in the distance and then heard the rumbling of the approaching train. She pressed her face against the ground, terrified, as the train screamed past her, shaking the ground. After it thundered past, she raised her head and saw the children dart up to the tracks, searching excitedly in the dirt for something.

One of the boys reached to the ground and straightened up, hollering, "I found it! I found it!"

He clutched this unknown treasure high above his head, and the other children rushed to inspect it.

Yoon Myoung had become lonely, and she desperately wanted someone to be near. Mustering her courage, she stood and slowly approached them. As she came closer, she thought, *They are so dirty! I've never seen children so ragged.* Should she come closer?

But her curiosity overruled her insecurities. She tiptoed silently toward them, staying as concealed as possible in the grass. She couldn't quite see what the boy held in his hand. So she crept closer, leaving for a moment her hiding place in the grass ...

The boy caught sight of Yoon Myoung. He first pointed at her with the thing in his hand, then clasped it tightly in his hand and pulled it back to his chest. But in that moment, she had seen that it was just a nail, a nail flattened by the wheels of the train.

The boy held his other fist up toward Yoon Myoung and shouted, "Tougee, tougee!"

She quickly scrambled down the embankment to hide again in the safety of the grass.

The children all joined in, chanting, "Tougee, tougee, tougee ..."

Yoon Myoung felt a heaviness spreading across her chest. Why did everyone call her tougee? What made her different from everyone else? No one else was a tougee, only her. She didn't understand. It felt like a stone deep inside of her.

What does it mean? she wondered. *Do I look worse than*

them? They are so dirty. They look like pigs. Am I worse than a pig, so that even the pigs insult me?

She ached for her mama's hugs, ached to bury her face in Sook Hee's comforting chest.

When Yoon Myoung peeked out of the grass a short time later, the children were moving east down the tracks, in the same direction Yoon Myoung must go. So she trailed a cautious distance behind them.

With the passing of another long day, darkness began to settle around her again. She watched the other children moving down the bank into the gully. Staying hidden, she did as they did. She could hear their muffled voices in the distance as they laughed. She was not willing to trust these newly discovered companions—even so, Yoon Myoung was consoled that she was not totally alone in the darkness.

She made her bed in the tall, stomped-down grass as she had the night before, lay on her back, and pulled the cloth up to her neck. Pulling up the shorter, young grasses near her, Yoon Myoung nibbled the roots and gazed up at the moon and the endless sea of stars. Her mind felt dull. Sleep finally overtook her.

A faceless man was lifting her high into the air, swinging her up and down ... her aunt snarled like a wild beast ... a child from her village poked at her with a stick ...

Startled out of the dream, Yoon Myoung whimpered, "Mommy!" but quickly realized where she was.

She felt for her mommy's lunch cloth and was about to pull it over her face when she detected five shadowy ghosts in the distant moonlight—the ragged children were worming their way up from the gully to the rail bed. They entered the tall grass on the other side of the train tracks, some of them crawling on their hands and knees while others slithered on their bellies. Yoon Myoung could make out a watchtower far ahead of them, standing alone in the moonlight, in the middle of a farmer's field. She knew that a hard-working farmer would be in the small hut built on stilts watching over his crops by night. She decided to follow.

She held back, staying low, not wanting to be seen. She watched as the children gathered their spoils and then crept back out of the field as they had come, escaping over the rails into the grass gully where they had made their beds. She could hear their hushed giggles as they gently struck melons on the ground, pulled them apart and slurped the sweet contents.

Yoon Myoung was excited by what she had just seen. *They took something from that farmer, and he doesn't know! I wonder if I can do that too?*

And yet she did not. Something inside her, a feeling, kept her from copying those children—at least on this night. She slipped silently back to her spot to return to sleep. But she had found out something new: She didn't have to be hungry anymore, if she could only accomplish for herself what she had just witnessed … the art of stealing!

CHAPTER 10

Play Day

The mountainous countryside, though war-torn, was dotted with picturesque villages. Golden mountains, checker-
boarded with lushly landscaped rice paddies, terraced into
the hillsides and filled the horizon. Yoon Myoung became
more at ease walking between the rice fields and along the
railroad ties. But she wondered how long her ride on the
black dragon could have been. After many days of wandering, seeing one village after another, she still had not found
her mama. She became accustomed to the night sounds
and even the stray dogs that roamed the countryside.

"Here, doggie," she would call when she saw one in the
distance.

These pointy-eared, mangy creatures provided companionship and soothed her loneliness. Sometimes a dog
would curl up next to her in the dark. She found comfort
and warmth at the feeling of having one nestled next to
her feet.

Her discovery that she could steal from farmers was the
only thing that enabled her to feed herself. Yoon Myoung

learned to monitor the watchmen until they fell asleep, crawl noiselessly to the field on her belly, gently pluck the vegetables or fruit, scoot backward while keeping an eye out until she was far enough away to not be seen or heard, and then run until her heart felt like it would jump out of her chest.

The days melted into one another, as did the villages she left behind. Sunrise, sunset, food, and thoughts of Mama. The cycle continued.

⊶⊷

Every day, Yoon Myoung looked forward to seeing the black dragon, which rumbled by a few times a day. It seemed to be checking on her. Sometimes she tried to play hide-and-seek with it as it rattled by.

There was another game Yoon Myoung liked to play with the train, one she had learned by watching the other children. She had eventually crept close enough to them to discover what they were doing on the rails when her path first crossed theirs. Now when she discovered a discarded metal nail along the tracks, she cried, "Oh, goody! Another one!" as she tucked it into the lunch cloth tied around her head.

When she heard the rails humming with the sound of an oncoming train, she would carefully place the nail on the warm track. "It's coming!" she would say to no one while waiting to spot the billowing steam from the train's smokestack. "Hurry, hurry!" She would scramble down the embankment to wait.

When the last car had passed, she would run back up

to search in the gravel for her flattened treasure. "Where are you, little nail?" she would sing quietly. "I know you're here somewhere!" When she found it, she would cry, "Oh, here you are, you silly little thing!"

These pieces of metal became her friends.

"Hello, *Tokki*. How are you today?" She would make her voice light and airy as one nail would speak up to another.

"It's a pretty day today, *Sae*," replied the other one, Yoon Myoung's intonation changing to become the other nail character. "I am doing well, thank you. How are you?"

"Did you see the black dragon today?" Sae asked.

"The black dragon scares me," answered Tokki. "I stay hidden in my burrow until it passes."

"Oh, don't be afraid, little Tokki. The dragon won't hurt you. It's a shame you can't fly above it, as I can!" She hovered one nail above the other, as if it was in flight.

Yoon Myoung played with these "friends" for hours to pass the time. It allowed her to forget, for a short time at least, the hardships of being alone.

When she was not playing with her new friends, she used them in other ways. She smoothed the dust on the ground with the flat side and drew pictures with the point. She spent hours sketching the mountains, birds, and flowers that surrounded her. Yoon Myoung discovered that her flattened nails were sharp enough to cut vegetables and melons. Her collection grew over time. She saved every nail, any piece of metal, tin can—anything. There was a use for each discarded item she found. Once she found string and eagerly tied her treasures to bunches of tall grasses to watch them wave in the wind.

Now and then Yoon Myoung would come upon other war orphans. They were always mean to her, calling her names like pig or tougee. One group of orphans snatched her lunch cloth from her head, then grabbed her collection of nails and tin cans. Stolen, all of it!

"That's mine! Those are *my* friends!" she screamed after them. "My mama gave me that cloth! Give it back to me, you ... you ... tougee!" She chased them until she tripped and fell crying into the dirt.

Had she just used that word—that name everyone called her?

"Why did they take Mommy's cloth?" she whimpered helplessly. "Why don't they just go find their own? Why is everyone so mean to me?" She had lost her mother, her family, the soft blankets she had slept in each night, the rice-paper walls of her room. All she had left was a cloth and a handful of nails and scraps—and now she'd lost them too.

She wept, her face in her hands.

CHAPTER 11

The Foxhole

In the several weeks that had passed since Yoon Myoung found herself all alone on the train-station platform, she had passed a milestone without knowing it. She had turned five years old.

⁘

One morning, Yoon Myoung awakened to warm sunshine and a moist ocean breeze coming from the southeast. She lay in her grass bed on her back, her delicate, rounded hands cupped behind her head. Gazing up, she watched a bird soaring, drifting, then darting upward toward the white, billowing clouds. She sat up slowly and heard chirping crickets. There was a rustling in the tall grass around her. Gingerly parting the grasses with her hands, she discovered grasshoppers, spiders, and all sorts of other small creatures, hiding from the bird overhead. Yoon Myoung welcomed the company of the beetle that landed softly on her leg. She relished the freshness of a new country morning.

Yoon Myoung no longer liked to be surprised, nor did she like to surprise others. She peered slowly above the grasses to make sure she was alone. Finally, with caution, she rose to see what this new day would provide.

Gazing to the left, she saw the train tracks running along the rugged mountains and knew that her home must be over there somewhere. She looked to the right, the way she had come, and scanned the train tracks surrounded by grass, rice paddies, and more mountains. Turning, she saw behind her only empty countryside, and even more mountains in the distance.

She squinted ahead.

On the horizon she could make out a familiar-looking object. "*Namu!* That looks like my village tree!"

Each small village had a stately tree, often a ginkgo tree, its broad crown spreading widely over the area. These deeply rooted trees were the center of activity in the villages.

Yoon Myoung began to run.

Her little legs ached by the time she approached the spreading branches. As she drew near, her heart sank with the realization that this tree stood alone, with no village surrounding it. The enormous golden tree was deserted.

Hearing the bubbling of water, she was immediately distracted and scampered toward a creek. She pulled off her shabby clothing and splashed in the cool water. Giggling and laughing, she spent the entire day exploring the stream. She lay in the mire along the side of the creek and patted her skinny legs with the thick sludge. After waiting for the silt to settle, Yoon Myoung rinsed herself and her threadbare dress, hanging it on a low branch to dry. Stretching out naked on a large, flat boulder, Yoon Myoung pulled some of the marshy grass reeds along the edge of the water, roots and all, and nibbled while the sun tickled her with its warmth.

When the setting sun began to hide behind the purple mountains, Yoon Myoung decided to stay there for the night. She made herself a bed under the tree, next to the running water. She liked this day. She lay down and looked up to the evening sky, which had turned many kinds of red, and covered herself as well as she could with grass reeds. Her eyelids fluttered shut with the thought that tomorrow she would find her mama.

✦✦

The cool hint of autumn awakened Yoon Myoung. When she sat up, she was drawn to beautiful red, white, and pink blossoms that flowered on the bushes nearby. Stepping toward the shrubs, she balanced on her toes to reach an especially bright flower. She placed the entire bloom on her tongue and sucked the sweet nectar. Although surprised by its toughness, she chewed the petals up hungrily.

"This is really yummy," she exclaimed each time she popped one into her mouth.

Though she still desperately wanted to find her mama, Yoon Myoung was becoming accustomed to this new life of isolation. She watched the wind sweep up and down the mountainside, leaving a trail as it brushed the rice fields on its journey to another mountaintop. The grasses swayed delicately. Yoon Myoung imitated them, letting her body dance to the rhythm of the grasses and the breeze. She giggled with delight as she lost herself in rhythmic movement.

"I wonder what's up there," Yoon Myoung said and decided to hike to the crest of the hill and find out.

The wind pushed against her scrawny body as she climbed. At the top, she surveyed all that was below, her new vantage point making her feel bigger. She saw the tree where she had spent the night. She lay down to play her favorite game with the white clouds against the blue afternoon sky.

"Look, there's a kitty. And there's a cricket. There goes a mean dragon!"

The grasses were tall enough to protect Yoon Myoung, so she ended another magical day by staying on the top of the hill for the night.

⇥⇤

Walking through the golden stalks in the rice fields a few days later, she scared up long-legged grasshoppers that clung to her, startling her. They were twice as big as Yoon Myoung's largest finger! She grabbed for one and caught it but quickly let it go when its strong hind legs pushed powerfully against her hands, tickling her. She caught another, this time holding it tightly. When she caught it, she had no idea what she might do with it—but her gnawing, cramped belly gave her an idea.

"I wonder what this would taste like," Yoon Myoung said out loud. "It might be good."

She stunned it between her palms and popped it quickly into her mouth. It crunched in her teeth and squirted out juice that she found not too unpleasant, encouraging her to try another. The few she ate didn't fill her grumbling tummy, but she was glad that she'd found another source of food.

She recalled that when she'd seen villagers bring in fish from the sea, they would lay them out to dry before eating them. So she captured many grasshoppers and strung them wriggling on a rice reed, allowing them, too, to dry out. After many hours of catching and stringing them, she proudly hung the numerous strings of fat grasshoppers around her waist with her other treasures.

Each day Yoon Myoung waited as long as she could before nourishing her angry stomach with her one daily meal. If anything was left over, it became breakfast the next day. Grasshoppers became a delicacy.

⤜⤛

The days were becoming shorter and the nights even cooler. It had begun to rain, which made the trails slippery with mud.

One chilly morning, Yoon Myoung was awakened by her body's violent shivering. She was wet all over from the rain that had fallen overnight. "Oh no!" she gasped, "I'm soaking wet!" Wringing the moisture out of her dress she wondered, *How can I stay dry when it rains like this? I must find my way home, so the roof will keep me dry and my blankets will keep me warm!* Yoon Myoung stood and scanned the hillside. Grass and mountains—and there, black in the dim, cloudy dawn, the train tracks that would lead her back home.

She settled against a tree trunk and drew her knees up to her body, hugging them to keep herself warm. She felt reassured knowing that the rails were still there to guide her way—though they would keep her no warmer. And no dryer.

She sat only a few moments before standing and striding down the hill, through the grass, away from the tree that had sheltered her and back to her journey on the tracks.

⁕

Several times Yoon Myoung had discovered holes dug out of the hillside. Her mama had told her soldiers used the holes as shelters from enemy fire during the war. Now, when she found them, she would burrow deeply into the hole at night to keep out of the biting cold wind that had picked up in recent days. Yoon Myoung had never been exposed to such chilling weather. Shivering uncontrollably all night, she whimpered for her mama while trying to stay covered with the grasses and reeds that made up her nest in the earthen cleft.

Awakening one morning to a blanket of snow, she first peered out of the hole, then tried to lift her stiff, weak legs. She could—but barely. Her bones ached. The clouds parted, and the sun began to shine, painfully bright on the snow, as she tried to limber up her stiff legs. Then she crawled out of her hole.

I have to find a village, she thought. *Somebody will help me there.*

She stumbled down the hillside, thinking that the next

village must not be far. As she trudged through the snow, she could no longer feel her feet.

She was surprised to see a flash of light a few feet in front of her. *Perhaps another treasure*, she thought.

She veered toward the sparkle and brushed away the snow to find a large, flat piece of shiny metal. As she pulled it from the ground, the snow dropped into a sizable foxhole that had been dug into the hillside and hidden by the sheet of metal and overgrown by grass. This foxhole was much larger than any others she'd seen. Instinctively, Yoon Myoung dove into the shelter and scooted all the way in, where immediately the sharp wind ceased nipping at her skin, even though the raw chill remained.

Yoon Myoung remembered how warm and soft her beds in the grass had been during warmer weather. Reluctantly, she emerged from her tiny cave and searched hurriedly for some grass to cover herself with. She found some barren stalks and shook away the snow, then tugged the grasses from their roots and dragged them to her burrow. She piled them in and packed them down. She pulled the metal sheet over the entrance to the hole and crawled, exhausted, into bed.

This is my very own little nest, she comforted herself. *Maybe I can stay warm in here.*

But she was not warm. She was, in fact, dreadfully cold. Still, she remained safe and dry.

❦

Sometime during the night, the cold wind awakened her, whipping across the mountainside and in and out of her hideaway. The metal door could not keep out the wind. She was shaking uncontrollably. She needed something to stop the cutting air from blowing in. Terrified of what the cold and the shaking might do to her body, Yoon Myoung crawled out of her shelter into the moonlit night. Picking her way carefully down the trail, she soon spied the faint shadows of lantern lights in the village below. In just a few minutes she stood outside the first hut. It was dark and quiet.

Wild-eyed and panicky, Yoon Myoung looked for anything to wrap around her body. She saw nothing but a rice-reed mat hanging on the porch. Yoon Myoung furtively helped herself to it and scurried away.

This will be a better door for my nest.

But when she'd returned to her foxhole and put the mat in place, the wind and snow beat against the rice-reed entry. The rocks and sticks she used to keep the mat in place failed. She tried repeatedly to prop up the straw barrier, but it continued to come loose.

"Stupid wind!" she yelled at the nighttime darkness.

Angrily giving up, Yoon Myoung yanked the rice-reed mat into the little cave and wrapped it around her body. She squirmed headfirst into the burrow with the rice-reed mat wrapped around her and the grass and reeds piled around her feet.

Yoon Myoung's trembling finally subsided.

"It will be all right," she assured herself, using her mama's parting words. "I am safe here."

CHAPTER 12

The Kitchen Miracle

At first Yoon Myoung did not venture far from her new home. Her nighttime visits to the village happened only when she needed to scavenge food and supplies. Sometimes, though, she heard the cries of playing children and would sneak down the hill to watch them until the cold drove her back to the foxhole. She knew that, for reasons she didn't understand, she wouldn't be welcomed in the village, so she kept a safe distance.

During the numbingly cold winter days and nights, Yoon Myoung would listlessly lie in her burrow and think about her mama.

I miss Mommy ... Does she miss me? Is she looking for me? How will she ever find me? she brooded.

❦

One day, feeling more courageous, Yoon Myoung approached a small home on the outskirts of the village and pressed her body against the warm kitchen wall. She watched the mother of the house go about her daily chores:

hanging wash in the frigid weather, gathering sticks for fuel, sorting red peppers for an evening meal. Although Yoon Myoung was trying to not be spotted, the woman occasionally glanced her way.

But she's not shooing me away, thought Yoon Myoung. *She doesn't call me tougee. Maybe she doesn't see me.*

The woman's long black hair was braided down her back, like Yoon Myoung's mother's hair. She didn't talk loudly or move briskly like the other village women did. She made her chores look beautiful.

She looks like a princess. Yoon Myoung's heart beat a little faster.

She drew her arms tightly around her body.

For several days, Yoon Myoung came to the warm wall to be near this princess.

Maybe the nice lady would like to be my mommy, dreamed the little girl. *Maybe she will take care of me.*

One night Yoon Myoung left her burrow, desperate to trust the tenderness she had felt from the mother in the village. She stumbled in the dark down the familiar path to the village and stopped outside this woman's hut. Creeping soundlessly, so as not to awaken anyone, she moved closer.

"Shh," she whispered to her hammering heart. "Keep quiet!"

The small kitchen was connected to the house. Lower than the rest of the house, the kitchen's earthen kiln doubled as a heater. The coal burning in the oven warmed the floor, heating the occupants in their rooms. Yoon Myoung noticed that the wooden door to the kitchen was slightly ajar. Heart still pounding, she quietly pushed open the door. It creaked ever so slightly. She paused, and when it seemed that no one had heard her, she looked around until she was sure that no one was in the kitchen. The clay stove warmed this small, dirt-floored area with brightly burning coals. A large iron pot filled with water sat on the stove. Yoon Myoung found a ladle and drank some of the warm liquid.

Oh, it had been so long since such warmth had gone down her throat. Her chilled bones began to thaw as her body warmed from the inside out. She scraped the bottom of the barley pot, finding a few remnants from the evening meal.

It feels so good in here, Yoon Myoung thought, sighing. *I'm going to stay here forever!*

She spent the night huddled on the hard floor next to the clay stove.

Yoon Myoung was awakened by coughing coming from inside the house. Dawn was about to unfold, and fearful she would be seen, she crawled gingerly to the kitchen door on her knees. A man was leaving the hut, wood-framed rucksack on his back. She had to leave before anyone found her! Stopping just long enough to help herself to some straw from the thatch of the roof, she quietly slipped out and headed back to her burrow with a bounce in her step. She didn't cry all day.

Maybe the mother left the door open for me. Yoon Myoung took it as a kindness intended especially for her. She returned that night. And the night after.

That kitchen became her lifeline, the miracle that enabled her to survive her first Korean winter.

CHAPTER 13

Survival

Every morning at dawn, Yoon Myoung reluctantly left the warmth of the kitchen in the village to return to her foxhole, where lethargy would put her back to sleep. On clear days when she felt a little energetic, she searched for grass sticking through the snow. She hoarded frozen roots along with the bark of trees.

Rice straw from the fields had become necessary for survival. She didn't remember learning the art of weaving these long strands together, but when her shoes wore out, she instinctively knew what to do. Braiding these straws together tightly, she discovered how to make a basket weave thick enough for the bottom of her feet. She added more straw as a tie to connect the woven soles to her feet. As the temperatures dropped further, she pressed more and more straw against her skin and then entwined it around her arms and legs with her longest strands. This layer from nature would keep her partly protected from the outside elements.

Eventually, Yoon Myoung had scavenged all the edible

plants within the vicinity of her hole. On her path to the village, she had noticed tiny tracks in the fresh snow from some sort of small animal. One day, she saw out of the corner of her eye the quick movement of a light gray field mouse, disappearing into its hole. She crawled to the furry creature's tunnel, squatted next to it, and waited. Her patience paid off when the mouse stuck his nose out and then stepped out a bit farther. Yoon Myoung grabbed its head and was promptly nipped on the finger.

She let the rodent go with a quick "Ouch!" and watched it disappear back down its hole. She stubbornly decided this mouse was going to be her supper.

She remembered the small bamboo traps she had seen in her home village. *Could I make something to trap it?*

Using her flattened nails, she cut and sawed pieces of twigs and reeds she had gathered and wove them together in the same way she had created her shoes. Her persistence paid off—soon she had a snare.

Yoon Myoung located several holes in the snow-covered rice field and placed her trap carefully and quietly over one. She backed up, squatted in the snow, and waited.

"Come, little mouse," she whispered. "I know you're in there … "

Just as Yoon Myoung had begun to fear that her hard work was in vain, the trap jumped into the air!

"I did it!" she shouted, then looked around to make sure no one from the village had heard.

She had learned from the chomp on her finger earlier to approach this little mouse differently. Yoon Myoung opened the trap door very slowly, then quickly grabbed the rodent and gave its head a sharp twist. The mouse lay motionless in her hand. Holding it by the tail, she scurried back to her burrow. With her nail, she ripped the stomach open and pulled out the innards.

"Yuck!" she groaned.

She skewered the mouse on another nail and held it over the live coals she'd carried in a tin can from the warm kitchen that morning. Burning off as much fur as she could, she devoured the entire creature including its gristly tail. Tiny Yoon Myoung didn't need much to appease her ever-present hunger.

⇥⇤

On most nights, the kitchen door remained ajar, but occasionally Yoon Myoung would find it tightly secured.

She would panic. *There has to be another place I can go to stay warm!*

A desperate Yoon Myoung explored other huts around the village. One such night, on the opposite edge of the village, she stumbled upon a mud-walled structure with only three walls. It was different from the homes in the village.

Despite the unfamiliar stench that lingered in the air, Yoon Myoung wondered, *Maybe I could live here? Would the villagers let me? I would stay out of their way.*

As she explored this newfound shelter, the moonlight revealed dark stains against the purity of the snow. She strained her eyes to make out what these stains were— until suddenly their deep-red color revealed that they were blood. Terror gripped her. What was this place? What had happened here?

As she turned to flee, she saw something sticking out of the snow. Frightened as she was, she was also intrigued. Warily, she moved closer to this twisted, black twig-like thing and noticed that it was covered with hair. Afraid to touch it but full of curiosity, she reached out and quickly tapped it, then jumped back swiftly. It didn't budge, so she did it again, this time with a sudden tug. The thing emerged from the snow! The tail from a butchered pig!

Yoon Myoung fled to her burrow with her find. Attempting to thaw it out, she laid on the curly treasure all night. By morning, it had softened. Yoon Myoung gnawed on it, spitting out the bristly hair while getting through the skin to the gristle. This delightful treat occupied her entire morning.

Checking the slaughter hut became part of Yoon Myoung's nightly prowl. Because meat was precious to these poor villagers, she usually found only carcasses that had been scraped clean. But occasionally she would find tails and sometimes bones. She learned that if she gnawed on the bones long enough, she could crack them open and get to the marrow.

One night, she arrived at the hut to find a village dog digging his way through the snow. She knew better than to compete with the fierce teeth that snarled possessively back at her. Yoon Myoung withdrew dejected and hungry, returning to her den.

The sun had begun to make more frequent appearances. One sunny afternoon, Yoon Myoung returned empty-handed from trapping. Frustrated, she fell onto her straw floor with an exhausted sigh, only to leap back up in shock.

"Oh, the snow is melting!" cried the child. "I can't stay here in this wetness. My things will be ruined!"

Yoon Myoung quickly gathered her tin can, nails, and straw mat. Reluctantly, she left the foxhole burrow that had been her home, and encased in layers of straw plaits, looking like a scarecrow, she wandered the outskirts of the village. Eventually, she found a temporary shelter under the eaves of an oxen shed at the edge of the village.

CHAPTER 14

Mudang

Miraculously, Yoon Myoung had survived her first winter. Her keen senses had taught her to use every resource that had been available around her. A cold, crisp chill, however, haunted the early spring air.

One day, Yoon Myoung crouched alongside the rough lean-to, spying on the village. She was still dressed in her layers of disintegrating straw, but she was not as cold in them now as she had been just a few days before. The season was turning.

In the village, each home had its doors wide open, and the women were all sweeping out dirt. They chattered among themselves above the scraping of their stick brooms.

"So many deaths this past winter!"

"Yes, it has been a difficult year."

"We must have the *mudang* visit to change our fate and invoke good spirits for spring."

Another festival? hoped Yoon Myoung. She was warmed

by just the memory of the festive spirit in her home during Chuseok, when she had scampered around with her cousins in her pretty striped jeogori. But the memory was now bittersweet.

Several days later, Yoon Myoung awoke to the beating of drums and clanging of bells. She peered around the corner of her lean-to shelter. In the center of the village, a woman dressed in a multicolored robe thrashed wildly, chanting in slurred, deep tones. A shaman mudang! She spun, danced, beat on drums fastened to her body, and fell to the ground, releasing control of her body to an animal spirit. Unable to resist, Yoon Myoung took a great risk and drew closer, right behind the villagers. Squatting on all fours, she peered between their legs. As Yoon Myoung watched the shaman rolling in the dirt, her feverish eyes suddenly met those of Yoon Myoung. To Yoon Myoung's alarm, the mudang leaped to her feet and charged. The crowd drew back, leaving her exposed and unprotected. Yoon Myoung's mind screamed, "Run!" But she was frozen, unable to move. The shaman pushed Yoon Myoung's head into the earth with one hand and with the other she began to thrust a huge butcher knife into the air above Yoon Myoung, swinging it back and forth as if attacking an invisible enemy. Three times, the crazed mudang filled her mouth with a dipperful of water and spewed it out upon Yoon Myoung, declaring, "Spirits be gone!"

Although at first Yoon Myoung had been terrified, too frightened to feel anything else, soon she grew angry. Who was this woman who held her face in the dirt and spat water upon her? Her mother would never have allowed anyone to do this to her! With all the strength her weak, frightened body could muster, she wiggled free of the shaman.

"Don't hurt me!" she choked out, shaking violently. "Leave me alone!"

Yoon Myoung's unexpected movement knocked the woman off balance. Her knife swung wildly as she fell, and she sliced Yoon Myoung's chin, from which blood immediately began to spurt. A hush fell over the crowd.

The shaman struggled to her feet, then soberly slid the knife into the folds of her robe. "The dirty spirit has been cleansed from your village," she proudly announced.

Suddenly, the kind lady who left her kitchen open at night was standing beside Yoon Myoung. She lifted her off the ground, pulled off her own head cloth, and pressed the scratchy gauze cloth firmly against the gash on Yoon Myoung's chin with strong, gentle hands that reminded Yoon Myoung of her mama's. It had been so long since Yoon Myoung had been held in anyone's arms. This woman was so tender. A warm, light feeling spread through Yoon Myoung.

When the bleeding stopped, the woman carefully wrapped the thin fabric under Yoon Myoung's chin and tied it on top of her head. Despite the warm feeling, Yoon Myoung could only stare into the distance, empty and lost.

Something important had happened. Yoon Myoung didn't understand why, but she knew she could not stay here any longer. It was as if a spell had been cast on her.

Yoon Myoung rested in her rough oxen shed until the weak, late-winter sun had climbed to its noon height, and then she rose and walked away from the village, feeling numb. The shaman's evil grimace flashed into her mind over and over, stabbing her with sorrow and heaviness.

CHAPTER 15

Field Work

Yoon Myoung spent the next several days following the tracks, hoping every hour to see her village tree come over the horizon and finding shelter and food where she could. The spring sun grew warmer each day. Yoon Myoung noticed life sprouting along her path. She plucked the baby grasses that peeked through the thawing snow so she could suck their fragile roots.

Winter had taken a toll—Yoon Myoung was thin, weak, and uncomfortable. "These sores hurt," she said, noticing the red welts and open boils that had begun to cover her scrawny body. "And I'm so dirty! My head itches, my body itches ... everything itches." She remembered that her mama had often searched through Yoon Myoung's hair to pick out the eggs of lice so that her hair wouldn't become infested with the minute creatures—but it had been a long time since anyone had picked lice and their eggs from her hair. That, no doubt, was why her head itched so badly. It had been just as long since her hair had been brushed—

Yoon Myoung couldn't even run her fingers through it anymore, it was so matted.

"I must get this straw off me … but what will I put on?" No clothing was ever left outside for her to steal, and the hay mats she had woven to cover herself were falling apart.

⇥⇤

The farmers she passed were plowing and preparing their fields for barley and rice planting. The starter shoots were wheeled in large burlap bundles to the side of the fields. It was there that Yoon Myoung found something to wear.

"This will work," she announced excitedly, when she discovered one of the sacks that had been left behind. She looked anxiously all around—no one was in sight. She snatched it and ran for cover behind the tracks.

Settling into a cozy, hidden nook warmed by the sun, she used one of her nails to cut a neck hole in the top of the sack and two holes in the sides for her arms. With delight, Yoon Myoung reached her arms through the bag and slipped it down over her head.

Exhilarated by her find, she began to run—yet something wasn't right. The burlap felt like needles scraping against her delicate skin. "Oh, my new dress is so scratchy!"

Spying a creek up ahead, she thought, *If I get it wet, maybe I can soften it.*

She scrubbed and pounded the sack with a rock in the creek, then laid it out to dry. After it stopped dripping, she put on the damp sack dress.

"Stupid thing! It still itches!"

Yanking it off again, Yoon Myoung crouched in the freezing water and washed and scrubbed the cloth over and over. This time she beat it on the rocks until she was worn out. She left it to dry without a watchful eye while she rested. After a few hours, she again tried it on. This tent covering was still a bit stiff, but it had lost its sting.

Still—it was so plain. How could she make it pretty?

Weaving grass together to make a belt, she tied it around her waist. Yoon Myoung looked down at the belted sack and thought it looked prettier this way—it also kept out some of the breeze, and she felt warmer. She found that she could mash flowers against the mesh to stain the rough fabric with color.

"This is much better!" Yoon Myoung was pleased with this new dress.

❧

One day, as Yoon Myoung came around a rock ledge on a mountain trail, she nearly collided with a farmer. They were both startled.

The farmer grabbed Yoon Myoung and shook her. "You dirty orphan—stealing my food! If you steal, you must work."

Yoon Myoung was confused. She hadn't stolen the farmer's food! Not this farmer, anyway. She stumbled along the trail as he pulled her roughly by the arm to a rice paddy.

"I need you to work in my field today," he barked at her. "The rice starts must be planted, and I need all the help I can get!"

Frightened by the gruff man and still confused, Yoon Myoung just stared at him.

"Go on—get busy!" he scolded. "I will give you a bowl of barley soup after you finish."

Eager for a bowl of hot barley soup, Yoon Myoung got to work. She worked hard alongside the farmer and the other members of his family, pushing the small rice plants into the mud. The sun warmed her even while the mud chilled her feet. After several hours, her back began to ache from bending over. The day dragged on. Eventually, the farmer's wife motioned for her. Yoon Myoung approached the woman, who knelt beside a small fire of charcoal, over which hung a pot. The woman poured some soup into a bowl and motioned to Yoon Myoung to sit.

"Here—eat," she said coldly. "You have worked hard."

As Yoon Myoung sat on the ground and crossed her legs, eager to taste her soup, she gasped. Leeches were attached by their little sucking mouths all over her feet and legs! She nearly spilled her soup, then steadied it. She'd thought about this soup all day, and even these bloodsuckers wouldn't deter her from eating it.

It had been two complete seasons since Yoon Myoung had eaten a full bowl of soup. The rich flavor brought back memories of her mama. She wished her mama was here to take care of these ugly leeches, which were puffing up with her blood before her very eyes. Then she noticed the other workers gently pulling the leeches from their legs. Setting her empty bowl in the grass, she pulled on one of the slimy things, but it wouldn't release.

One of the women noticed Yoon Myoung's predicament and motioned for her to watch while she sprinkled white powder on the back of one of the leeches. It wriggled for a moment or two and then loosened its grip. Then the woman stretched out her hand to offer the little girl some powder. Yoon Myoung drizzled the white magic on the fattest leech on her leg and watched it sizzle until she could pop it off. Only a red welt remained. One by one, she sprinkled the powder on each black, slimy enemy until they all had been destroyed. All that remained were red blotches covering her legs and feet.

For several days, Yoon Myoung stayed near the rice fields and worked during the day in anticipation of an evening bowl of hot soup and some tea at dawn. When night fell, Yoon Myoung would climb on top of a dirt berm, pull her arms, legs, and head inside her sack dress, and wrap her arms around herself like a blanket.

One dusk, Yoon Myoung stood above the rice paddies and realized that all of the starts had been planted. There would be no more soup. It was time to move on. It was time to go to her mama.

CHAPTER 16

The Waterwheel

The next day started well. Springtime sunshine warmed Yoon Myoung's body as she walked. She loved being warm again. The sweet aroma of new flowers drifted up the mountain trail. Yoon Myoung listened to the insects in the tall grasses and heard an occasional bird calling in song. Although she was still walking along the railroad tracks, she had no idea where she was. But the rolling mountains, lush valleys, and rice paddies filled with light-green shoots and grasses felt familiar and soothing to her.

There was one thing that was not comfortable. As the day wore on, the growling in her tummy grew louder, and the hunger pains became so strong that she could think of nothing else. She had to find something to eat.

Wandering beside a rice field with a village in the distance, Yoon Myoung noticed some of her little black enemies lying in the mud beneath the water's surface. They no longer frightened her, so she reached down to pluck one from the base of a rice stalk and place it on a rock in the sun. She found a few more and then smashed them all with a small stone. Could this be a source of food? Scraping the ooze from the rock with her index finger, Yoon Myoung licked the goop, gagged it down—and instantly began to heave.

She made a firm resolution: It didn't matter how hungry she was, these slimy leeches would never tempt her again.

The convulsions of her stomach after trying to eat leeches made her hunger pains even worse, and Yoon Myoung sank onto the path, covering her head with her hands. She wept tearlessly.

She would have to enter the village.

Yoon Myoung approached new villages cautiously and almost always after the sun had set. But she remembered the motherly kindness of the village woman whose kitchen Yoon Myoung had shared and her recent experience with the field workers. Maybe there would be others like them?

Yoon Myoung carefully circled to the back of the village and hid behind a crumbling stone wall. She watched the women and children around the well. Seeing and hearing the rhythm of happy village life filled her with a longing for home. *Will I ever see my mama again? I miss her so much … and I'm so hungry.*

The homes at the edge of the village seemed quiet. Yoon Myoung waited. Noticing that there was no activity at one of the huts, she crept along the stone wall toward it until she came to an opening. From her new angle, she glimpsed red peppers hanging from strings and vegetables hanging from the front eave of the porch to dry. They were too high to reach, but Yoon Myoung could also see a stool in front of the house. She looked around one more time to see if anyone was watching, then dashed to the stool and dragged it beneath the eave. Standing on it, she stretched on her tiptoes toward some spring onions. She had just wrapped her hand around the prize when she heard a shout from behind her.

"What do you think you are doing, you dirty thing?"

Startled by the loud yell, she tumbled from the stool. Springing up, she snatched the vegetables and began to madly scramble toward the opening in the wall—but then her body was quickly whipped backward. She gasped for breath. The farmer had an unrelenting hold on her sack dress, and he grasped her so tightly he was choking her.

"You dirty, filthy tougee! How dare you come into my yard? I have my own family to feed."

"I'm sorry! I'm sorry. Here—you can have it back."

Yoon Myoung stretched out her shaking arm, trying to hand back the cluster of onions.

The farmer threw her down into the dirt, the onions scattering about her. "You're disgusting, you little pig!" he shouted, drawing the attention of nearby villagers.

She tried to get up, but he knocked her down again with the back of his hand, this time striking her across her face.

"Please don't hurt me," Yoon Myoung pled. "I will leave. I won't come back. Just let me go."

A crowd was now gathering, adults and children alike. *Is there any kind person here*, she wondered while searching the faces of the crowd, *someone who will stand up for me, someone who will protect me?* She could see only hatred, anger, and disgust on the faces of the villagers.

The farmer grabbed the back of Yoon Myoung's burlap and lifted her up from the ground with a calloused hand. He glared at her and then slowly looked over at the others who had gathered.

"If we don't do something with this tougee," he snarled, "she will steal *your* food too. We must get rid of her."

Yoon Myoung screamed, "Please, please let me go! I am sorry. I will work for you. I won't steal from you again. Please don't hurt me!"

A woman's voice cried, "Let her go! She's just a child. She didn't take your food—it's still there, on the ground."

Another voice shouted, "Get rid of her! She's a thief. She will come back and steal again!"

A child began to cry. Some of the older children added their voices to the crowd: "Get rid of her!"

A few argued, "Let her go." But the farmer waved a hand dismissively, his face still angry. He motioned for some of the men to come.

One stepped forward and grabbed Yoon Myoung's wrist while another gripped her other forearm. Her feet dragged on the ground, over rocks and stones, as the men pulled her along a path up a hillside. Her body clenched tightly with fear.

"Where are you taking me?" she screamed. "Please let me go! I said I'm sorry. I will leave if you just let me go!"

Yoon Myoung was more frightened than she had ever been. These people hated her so much—it could not have been just because she tried to steal some onions.

The men dropped Yoon Myoung on the rocky ground. She tried to scramble away, but a hand thrust her face into the dirt. She heard the sound of sloshing water—the churning of a waterwheel, somewhere behind her. Weathered hands again clasped her arms. Others grabbed her legs. She was lifted back into the air.

Adrenaline flooded her. "What are you doing, you ... you ... filthy pigs!" She thrashed and screamed. "Let me go! Let me go! What are you doing?"

She soon found out. The men thrust Yoon Myoung roughly against the waterwheel, banging her head against it. The rough wood scraped her back, and her head throbbed. They stretched her arms high above her head, making her shoulders ache so that she cried out in pain, and lashed them to the wheel, cutting off circulation in her wrists. Her ankles were cinched to the wheel's sides with braided rope. She twisted and turned, trying everything in her power to wriggle free of this nightmare. A backhanded slap to the face stopped her writhing.

"Please stop! You're hurting me!" she screamed. "Mommy, Mommy, help me!"

She looked among the small group of farmers who were standing by, looking for someone who might help her. But one by one, some of them with looks of embarrassment or shame, others laughing uneasily, they shuffled away, until only the farmer who had first caught her and the other man who'd carried her to this place remained.

The farmer pushed a lever that released the brake, and the creaking wheel gradually started to turn as the weight of the water spilled into each section. Yoon Myoung didn't quite know what was happening at first, except that she could feel the wheel moving. Its slow rotation took Yoon

Myoung to the top, where a flood of water spilled onto her face, causing her to sputter and choke. She thrashed her head from side to side to escape it. Then she began her descent on the other side, head first, her world turned upside down. With no time to catch her breath, she was thrust under the murky water as the wheel continued its rotation. Scraping along the gravelly bottom of the pond, she felt her face being cut and bruised by the mud and gravel. And after her face, the rest of her body—first her chest, then her knees. As her face came back out of the water, Yoon Myoung frantically spit and snorted out the rocky muck before wildly gasping for a breath of air.

Her shoulders ached as she was pulled back up to begin another cycle. The water assaulted her at the top of the circle once again, but this time she turned her head before it hit her eyes. Before she was submerged again, she grabbed a quick breath and closed her eyes. But nothing she did allowed her to escape the burning of her skin, her face being dragged through the gravelly mire below, while the rough wooden wheel tore at her back. The more she thrashed, the more the ropes holding her legs and arms bit into her flesh. The wheel continued to turn. Her mouth filled with something that was not water—blood, streaming down her face from the cuts there and now running into her mouth. She spit it out, then cried in agony, "Mommy! Mommy, please—save me! Save me!"

Each revolution of the wheel caused more pain, scraping her skin from her body. Gravel filled her nose and mouth. Her eyes swelled until she could not open them.

Suddenly the wheel stopped. Yoon Myoung hung limp

from her bonds, exhausted from fighting. A gentle arm lightly pressed against her; she felt the ropes that held her in this prison being released, one by one.

A man's voice, strong but kind, said, "I am not going to hurt you. I sent them away."

Yoon Myoung felt a strong arm lift her, then carefully place her weakened body on the ground. She still could not see, but she felt a moistened cloth gently cleaning the mud, gravel, and blood from her torn face and hair.

He then dried her with another cloth as he asked, "Little girl—little girl, can you hear me? Are you okay?"

Yoon Myoung mustered up the strength to nod her head—even though she knew she was not okay. The man put one large hand behind her head, then cupped her face with his other hand, tilting her face toward him. Making a great effort, she opened her swollen eyes and focused on his mouth.

"Little girl, these people want to hurt you. Listen to me. You must live. Live, little girl. You *must live!*"

He slowly rose and walked away. Yoon Myoung, too broken and weak to follow, lay there and watched him vanish around the side of the mountain. Longing arose in her heart. She wanted to run after him. She wanted to talk to him.

Please don't leave. Please help me. Why must I live? Do you know my mama?

But the man was gone. Her questions were left unanswered. Gradually, although her pain was still great, her strength came back.

I am not injured. I will try to catch up to him. He will help me.

She rose on her wobbly legs and moved in the direction the man had taken. She came to where he had disappeared, and beyond, but she wasn't able to find him.

That night as she lay in the tall grasses, as far from the bad village as her aching legs had been able to take her, trying to ignore the throbbing pain in her swollen face and head, the words of the man echoed in her head. "Little girl, you *must live!* Live, little girl. You *must live!*"

CHAPTER 17

Fireflies

Over time, the deep gashes on her arms and legs, the abrasions on her face—all the angry remnants of the villagers' cruelty—began to heal and scar. But harder than healing was trying to understand why the villagers had treated her that way.

"They are all so cruel," she said to herself. "They call me tougee. They want to hurt me. They might try to kill me. But the special man told me I must live. I *will* live."

⇥⇤

Late one afternoon, Yoon Myoung heard children's laughter in the distance. She carefully crept her way through the tall grass until she could see them on a hillside. A boy and two girls, laughing, were playing with the rim of a bicycle. They would push it down the slope and chase after it, trying to catch it. Then they would take the wheel back up to the top of the hill to do it again. She watched them for a long time, wanting to go join them, but she was afraid.

As dusk fell, she expected them to stop playing and

go to their families in the nearby village. But the children didn't leave. Yoon Myoung drew closer, still hidden by the grasses. One of the girls was dancing, twirling in circles. Something shiny sparkled over her head, as if fireflies were shimmering all around her. Yoon Myoung was mesmerized by the scene.

Over time the children quieted down. Yoon Myoung crept still closer, still low in the grass. She liked the feeling of having people near, and allowed herself to relax, to sink into her soft grassy bed. She closed her heavy eyes in the darkening evening, enjoying the soft voices of the children ...

Suddenly she found herself sitting up in fright, a sound echoing in her ears—and then realizing that the sound she'd heard was her own cry. She had drifted off into a dream, and the dream had become a nightmare—something she'd experienced more frequently lately. She heard soft footsteps running across the grass, and then there they were, the children, standing over her, whispering to each other as they stared at her. She instinctively curled into a fetal position to protect herself from being beaten.

But as she lay motionless in the moonlit dark, no blows came, no pain. Instead, the boy asked, "Who are you?"

Though she was still frightened, Yoon Myoung knew to show no weakness. "What does it matter to you?" she answered.

"This is our territory," the boy said.

"This is my mountain," Yoon Myoung said, trying to match his authoritative tone.

"What do you mean, 'This is my mountain'? Who told you this is your mountain?"

Yoon Myoung didn't answer.

"Where do you live?" he asked.

"Where do *you* live?" she said.

"We live anywhere we want."

"Well, I do too."

"Well, okay. Do you want to join up with us?"

One part of Yoon Myoung argued, *No, don't go. They might hurt you.* She ignored that voice, and rose and followed them. She settled into the grass a short distance from where the children had made camp. It was a strange comfort to her that these children had no home either. She allowed herself to fall asleep.

When daylight came, one of the girls poked Yoon Myoung awake.

"She looks strange," the girl said to the others. "What is wrong with her hair and eyes?"

"Her hair is curly."

"It's a funny color."

"Does it matter?" the boy said. "Leave her alone." He smiled at Yoon Myoung.

She glanced at him and looked down.

For the rest of the day, the pack of children—eight of them, counting Yoon Myoung—roamed and gathered food.

When the sun was high, they stopped to rest. Dumping a fistful of perfectly round and smooth stones onto the dirt, the boy with the smile challenged, "Can anyone beat me today?"

He tossed one stone in the air and with the same hand grabbed another stone on the ground. Then he tossed it again and grabbed two stones from the ground. He continued until he had picked all the stones in one turn.

"Aw," one of the others said. "That's not fair."

"Today is my day!" the boy laughed.

It felt good to Yoon Myoung to be with others.

That night, she solved the mystery of the dreamy lights. The children had scavenged tin cans with wire handles. Each of these cans had many tiny holes in the bottom and sides and contained hot embers of charcoal, snuck from fires in the villages. As the girls twirled their cans over their heads, the sparks flew out of the little vents! The children giggled and laughed. One of the girls offered her glowing charcoals to Yoon Myoung, who reluctantly extended her hand.

"Dance with it! Make us some fireflies!" they shouted.

Yoon Myoung slowly twirled and swirled. Enchanted by the magic twinkling, she began to giggle, to skip a little, and even join in the dance. She almost forgot that she was a tougee.

The next morning, the children awoke, gathered their meager belongings, and prepared to travel. They set out in the direction from which Yoon Myoung had been wandering. Yoon Myoung followed her new friends for several minutes—until she realized she might be led back to the waterwheel.

"I can't go with you," Yoon Myoung said.

"Why not?" one of the children asked.

"I just can't," she said. "Besides, I want to go this way." She pointed the other direction.

"Well, suit yourself," the boy said.

"Why don't you take this?" urged one of the girls, handing Yoon Myoung a pierced tin can with coals.

Gratitude washed over Yoon Myoung. "Thank you, thank you," she said.

The children walked on. Yoon Myoung turned and walked the opposite way, in the direction she hoped would lead her to home and her mama, occasionally glancing over her shoulder at her friends as they became smaller in the distance.

CHAPTER 18

Marketplace

It was summer again. Yoon Myoung had survived nearly four seasons since her mama had put her on the train and said good-bye. But that survival had come at a price. Yoon Myoung was now emaciated; her bones showed through her skin, and lice flourished in her matted hair. Her dirt-stained skin, never clean, was covered in boils—red, swollen areas that were painful to the touch. A number of scars testified to the harsh conditions she'd endured and the mistreatment she'd received. Yoon Myoung had become a wild child, with an air of defiance and nervousness, always on guard for danger. If her mother had passed her on the streets, she might not have recognized her own daughter.

⊶⊷

In the larger villages, throngs of people gathered in the open markets to barter their wares. Vegetables, fruits, all sorts of roots, and even chickens and fish were available for purchase or trade. Yoon Myoung had learned that the large crowds there provided a degree of safety, giving her the ability to go unnoticed. Most people were too preoccupied to watch children snaking through their legs—or even rifling through their foodstuffs. In these markets, she was usually able to get her hands on some kind of produce. Melons were her favorites, because she loved their juicy sweetness.

One morning, Yoon Myoung eyed a pile of yellow melons next to the butcher's stall. While the seller's back was turned, she snatched one and had just turned to dart out of the market when a strong hand grabbed her.

"You little tougee. What do you think you're doing?" growled the butcher, lifting her off her feet.

The melon dropped out of her hands and rolled up against the rickety counter of a vegetable booth. Dragging her to a wooden post near his stand, the butcher ripped off her sack dress, tore a piece from it, and tied her to the post.

"Let me go!" she shouted, thrashing and fighting.

"You're not going anywhere, you little thief," the butcher grunted. "This should teach you to stay away from now on."

Yoon Myoung's body throbbed with anger. She yelled again, "Let me go! Let me go! I hate you!"

"Oh … you hate me, do you?" he mimicked with a sneer, leaning down toward her. "You little tougee—"

Feeling her anger spin out of control, she mustered her strength and spat at her captor.

The man wiped it from his cheek in silence, then said quietly, through clenched teeth, "I'll show you what happens to tougees who do that." He turned to a cluster of children hanging around the market stalls, who had gathered to watch the excitement, and said, "Go fetch a stick. I want you to see what we do to a thieving dog!"

Two of the children ran off. Each returned in moments with a stick in hand. The other children watched as, at the butcher's direction, the two with sticks poked Yoon Myoung on her stomach and back.

"Don't! Stop it!" she shrieked. "You're hurting me! Leave me alone!"

"Hit the little tougee! She needs to be taught a lesson!" the butcher hissed, and with his encouragement, the two boys stopped poking and began to swing their sticks with all their might. Yoon Myoung had never been struck in this way—she tried to turn her body away from the blows, but when she avoided one boy's swings, the other would hit her from the other side. The sticks rained down on her shoulders, her legs, her ribs, and her head.

Villagers young and old walked by, shaking their heads. To Yoon Myoung, it seemed that they were mocking her during this public disgrace. Humiliated, she blocked out the pain of the blows and concentrated on breaking the burlap bonds that held her to the post. Finally, she tore away, seized her burlap rags from the dirt, snatched up the forgotten melon, and ran naked out of the market.

CHAPTER 19

Manure Pit

Yoon Myoung spent days hiding in the tall grass, nursing the wounds and bruises she'd received during the thrashing in the marketplace. She avoided anyplace she was likely to encounter other people and rationed the melon to make it last for several days.

Then one morning she heard young voices, and, investigating, she spied a group of children in a grassy meadow. She sat hidden in the grass, watching, gauging whether or not this group could be trusted. Were they like the children who had taught her to make fireflies and invited her to join them? Or were they like the children who had beaten her in the marketplace? They seemed rather wild, and she kept her distance. She was too far away to make out exactly what they were saying, but their voices were loud and their actions rough, pushing each other and arguing.

She lingered too long. One boy ran in her direction to retrieve an object one of the others had tossed, and his eyes lit on Yoon Myoung, even though she made herself small. Her heart raced when that boy called back to the others, and they all began running in her direction, waving their arms wildly and pointing at her. "Get her, get her!" they yelled.

Yoon Myoung leaped to her feet and fled, but her weary legs couldn't carry her fast enough. She glanced back over her shoulder as she ran—the oldest and biggest boy had pulled ahead of the pack. She had run only a few more seconds when he tackled her from behind. She hit the ground with a painful thud, his weight on top of her. He twisted her over onto her back and pinned her to the ground, his hands tightly grasping her wrists.

Yoon Myoung groaned, almost paralyzed by the searing pain caused by the fall, pain that moved up her back and into her head.

The rest of the children caught up, out of breath. They glared at her, and led by the oldest boy, apparently their ringleader, they began taunting.

"She's a tougee! A filthy, dirty tougee!" he scoffed.

"Tougee ... tougee ... tougee!" the others chanted.

How Yoon Myoung despised that word!

"I've just caught a *geseki*!" the older boy pronounced at his prize.

Yoon Myoung felt fear rising into her throat, but her stubbornness and anger would not let her plead with them. "You *deji*!" she snarled back.

"Don't call me a pig, you little tougee!"

The boy yanked her up off the hardened ground and held her tightly by her wrists. She tried to wriggle free of his grasp, but there were so many children in this gang, she knew she couldn't escape. The boy pulled her, all the others following, along the raised path that divided the rice paddies till they came to a large pit.

A foul odor filled the air as they approached. With a shock, Yoon Myoung realized that this pack of wild children was leading her to a fertilizer hole. In her fear, she screamed at the children insults and what curses she'd learned during the past year: "Let me go ... let me go ... you ... you pigs! You're all stupid dirty tougees ... all of you! Leave me alone!" She screamed until her voice grew hoarse. This fertilizer pit at the edge of the rice field, she knew, was where human waste from the nearby village outhouses would have been dumped.

Throughout, the children continued their taunting: "Tougee ... tougee ... tougee!"

When they reached the pit, the boy who held her lifted her, as she writhed desperately, above the sewage and dropped her feet first into the hole.

The excrement was like quicksand. It was so thick that Yoon Myoung couldn't even kick her legs to "swim" up to the top. She was being sucked into a bottomless hole. Looking up to the sky, she screamed. No words could come, just shrieks of agony.

"There you go, tougee! That's where you belong ... in the manure!"

The stench was unbearable. Yoon Myoung gagged. Struggling to keep her hands in the air, she was soon submerged up to her shoulders. She managed to lift her chin just enough to keep her face from sinking into the slurry. The more she wriggled, the farther down she sank. Eventually, the waste, infested by maggots, crept into her mouth. She gagged uncontrollably, overcome by sheer terror.

The older boy stooped next to the pit, cackling with delight. Finally satisfied with the panic and surrender he saw in her wild eyes, he held out a crooked stick. Yoon Myoung grabbed it and clutched as tightly as she could. He pulled her out of the mire, and she lay on her stomach in the matted grass at the edge of the pit.

Too weak to stand, still heaving, she heard one of the children start to sing. "Dirty little tougee, dirty as a deji…"

Soon all the children were chanting the rhyme. Her head spinning from the stench and from the filth on her body, she closed her eyes so that she wouldn't see her tormentors. But she could not escape their chanting—or the stench.

"Come on, let's get out of here," said the big boy. "Let's leave this smelly tougee alone." And they wandered away.

When she could no longer hear their laughter, Yoon Myoung slowly opened her eyes. She heard the sound of flowing water and crawled toward it. She found an irrigation ditch. She rolled in, even though the cold water shocked her skin.

Yoon Myoung understood. *I am just like this manure.* She tried to rub the filth from her body. "I am a tougee," she said. "A dirty little tougee."

⇥⇤

That night, Yoon Myoung held her knees tightly to her chest, rocking slowly back and forth. Her eyes burned as she fought the urge to cry. She gazed up blurry-eyed at the stars, and tried to remember her home—now just a distant dream. Despair had become her constant companion.

CHAPTER 20

"Ah beo ji?"

When the warm nights of summer had begun to turn cold again, and the leaves had begun to die and turn brown, Yoon Myoung found herself one morning hiding behind the tall, dry grass, watching a group of foreign soldiers standing near their big, green truck parked along the road. Although the war was over, from time to time Yoon Myoung saw these soldiers—or others like them—still helping the Koreans. Their trucks belched smoke that stung Yoon Myoung's eyes.

They were strange-looking men. Their skin was so light-colored and their faces so different, with pronounced jawlines and large, bony noses. Covered with hair, they seemed like giant monkeys to the smooth-skinned Yoon Myoung.

Whenever these strangers passed through a village, the children ran out to them, tugging on the soldiers' coats and trousers, begging for candy and food, shouting whatever English they knew.

"Hallo!"

"You allu monkey."

"Hey you, GI!"

"Love a you."

The soldiers laughed and often gave them something. At first, Yoon Myoung would watch these interactions from a distance. There once was a time, a soldier met her eyes. The giant approached her and knelt several feet away. She stepped back, ready to run. He reached into his pocket and pulled out a small package, which he extended to her. His eyes had gentle upward creases, and the smile on his face held her in place.

He spoke in a friendly voice. Yoon Myoung didn't understand anything he said, but he seemed kind, unlike the people in the villages. She wondered what was in the package he held out to her. She had seen other children eating what the soldiers gave them. She slowly extended her skinny hand, then abruptly pulled it back.

The soldier spoke again in his strange language, and again he seemed kind and reassuring. The softness in his voice made her lower her guard.

He inched a bit closer, still holding out this mysterious package. Yoon Myoung darted quickly forward, grabbed it out of his hand, and retreated beyond his reach.

The soldier laughed and spoke again. He made no move to come after her.

Feeling safely out of range and curious as to what this soldier had just given her, she stared at it for a moment, then pulled off the brown paper wrapper. Inside was a rectangular bar, lighter in color than its wrapping. She broke off a corner and carefully placed it on her tongue.

This sweet, creamy square melted on her tongue, causing her mouth to water. This was like nothing she'd ever tasted before. As the soldier walked away with a wave and a smile, she swirled it in her mouth while it dissolved and quickly popped in another piece, then another and another until it was all gone.

A short time later, Yoon Myoung's stomach started to spasm. Pain shot through her tummy in waves. The soldier's treat had been delicious, but she wished she had not eaten it all so quickly.

While suffering in a roadside ditch, Yoon Myoung's mind wandered back to a snapshot in time with her mother before her train ride.

They had passed two American soldiers while returning from the rice fields. Yoon Myoung grasped tightly her mama's hand, always a bit uncertain of these uniformed men. After the men had passed, Sook Hee paused on the dirt road and turned to look after them.

"Come on, Mommy. Why did you stop walking?"

"I'm sorry, Yoon Myoung. I was just thinking."

"Thinking about what, Mommy?"

Sook Hee waited a moment before saying, "Your daddy. I was thinking about your daddy."

"My daddy? Where is my daddy?"

Kneeling in front of Yoon Myoung, she stared deeply into her daughter's eyes. "Your daddy is like one of those soldiers," she said.

"A soldier? Where is he?"

"He is far, far away," Sook Hee explained. "He had to go back to his home in America. His family needed him there."

"Why?"

Sook Hee didn't answer.

"Mommy, why?" *repeated Yoon Myoung.*

"He just had to, my daughter."

"Is he coming back?"

"No, he's not. But I'm right here."

→←

Yoon Myoung had relived this memory many times. Now, hiding behind the grass watching the soldiers beside their truck in the road, she wondered: *Is one of these soldiers my daddy? But Mommy said he wouldn't come back—and now she is gone too!*

She shook off her sadness. Her mother had said her daddy had been a soldier. That meant that one of these soldiers might be her daddy.

Struggling against her shyness, she stood timidly and stepped toward the road. Several of the soldiers noticed her and smiled. One of them took a step toward her. She fought the urge to run. "Haro," she struggled.

Still smiling, the closest soldier answered in words she didn't understand.

"Ah beo ji?" she asked. Cocking her head, she pointed toward him.

The soldier seemed to understand her words. He shook his head, still smiling, then said in heavily accented Korean, "No, little girl, not your daddy. Like something to eat?"

The GI reached into his pocket, pulled out something shiny, and offered it to her. Distracted by the silver wrapper, she snatched it, tore it open, and smelled it. She had been sure it was the chocolate that had made her stomach sick, but this treat smelled like fruit, and she popped it into her mouth. It was sweet and juicy and made her mouth water. She continued to chew this mysterious treat, but was confused as to why it didn't go away in her mouth. So she just kept chewing—all day. That night she carefully placed the little wad on a rock by her head.

In the morning, although it had lost all flavor, she popped it back into her mouth. This time it was much harder and took more effort to sink her teeth into, but she chewed anyway.

The soldier's treat lasted for several days until it finally dissolved in her mouth.

He had given her a good treat.

But he was not her daddy.

CHAPTER 21

The Well

Fall came and went.

Miraculously, Yoon Myoung survived her second winter on her own. She searched out another large foxhole home near a village before the winter turned itself into a white monster. She gathered grass from the side of the mountains, took thatch from the fields, and stole another village hut mat for her door.

Remembering what she had learned the winter before, she wove coverings from thatch to keep her feet and body warm. She found access to another warm kitchen fire.

She endured. Every day brought the same exhausting challenge: outlast the winter. Her memories of home had blurred. What was real? What was not? All she knew for sure was that she was a tougee. A tougee with no home and no family.

Yoon Myoung did not even have a direction. One winter morning as she shivered in her foxhole, she realized with a shock that she had no idea where the train tracks were and didn't even remember when she'd followed them last.

That day she ventured out and explored the countryside around her foxhole. There were no train tracks—only the road she had followed to come to this place. How did I lose sight of them—and when? she wondered. She had lost the one thing—the only thing—that could lead her home.

From that day, she began to consider a terrifying possibility: that she would never find her way home.

†

The sun peeked above the hillside and Yoon Myoung pushed aside the woven mat curtain and crept stiffly from her foxhole home. The snow was gone, and the mud outside her foxhole had not frozen during the night—a sign that soon the grass shoots would begin emerging. Spring was almost here.

But winter had once again taken its toll. Her head was white from the lice eggs in her hair. She was constantly bothered by a variety of bugs and parasites living on her body, and she stank.

Drawing strength from the early spring warmth, Yoon Myoung peeled off her straw coverings. The sun felt so good—but even with her filthy, homemade clothes off, her skin itched, and she needed to scratch everywhere. And no wonder. Now that she was naked, she could see that her body was covered in red, oozing sores. She gathered a handful of fresh grass and tried to clean her sores. But that just irritated the boils and made them more inflamed.

"I'm on fire!" she cried. "What's happening?"

The more she rubbed her body with the dried grass, the more her skin burned and itched. She couldn't stand it—whatever it took to cure this burning, Yoon Myoung would do.

Water! She would clean her skin and soothe the burning.

But the closest water was in the well in the village.

All of her instincts, all of her experience, warned her to stay away from villages, except in the dark of night. But it was very early yet. Maybe no one would be near the well.

Yoon Myoung ran frantically toward the village, whimpering and scratching herself as she ran. As she had hoped, only a few small children played near the well. Yoon Myoung ignored them, grabbed the bucket, and threw it into the well to draw water.

"*Neo micheoseo!* Are you crazy?" said one of these village children.

"What's wrong with you?" said another.

"Why are you naked?" asked another.

"Leave me alone, you *babos!*" Yoon Myoung said.

But the cries of the children quickly brought their mothers. Yoon Myoung had no sooner pulled the bucket up and begun to rub her body with handfuls of cold water than she was surrounded by angry women. She tried to ignore them—the cold water did indeed, as she had hoped, soothe her burning skin.

"How dare you touch these children, you diseased pig!" shouted one of the women.

Yoon Myoung tried to keep scooping handfuls of water over her sores, but one of the women rushed at her. Yoon Myoung backed up and crouched, ready to fight. "You *deji!*" she hissed at the woman.

The woman spat at her and called over her shoulder. Soon a man appeared and grabbed for her shoulder. She tried to break away from him, clawing and scratching. She lunged for his hand, open-mouthed, and her teeth found flesh. Furious, he roared for more men, who quickly arrived. They gripped her flailing legs. She was caught.

Writhing, screaming, and cursing, she was no match for these strong farmers. Would they tie her to a waterwheel again? She tried to bite them too, but they were too strong. She went limp and waited to see what they would do.

"We can't let her stay here. She'll steal from us and infect our children. We need to get rid of her."

"Toss her in the abandoned well."

The man she'd bitten snickered. "That'll take care of her."

Yoon Myoung squeezed her eyes shut and felt herself floating over the ground as she was carried through the village, followed by the screams and insults of the women and children. When she felt herself being lifted up, Yoon Myoung opened her eyes—and looked down into a gaping, black well, dusty and filled with cobwebs. She could not see the bottom, only black distance. Terrified, she began to scream, begging the men to let her go. But they only laughed and hoisted her above the hole, letting her legs dangle. Once again, there would be no escape. Below her, only utter blackness.

They dropped her.

Spinning and thumping against the sides of the well, Yoon Myoung somersaulted until she splashed into the cold, numbing water. She'd been afraid, as she fell, that the well would be dry and that she would be smashed against the rocks. But the reality wasn't much better—the well had been abandoned for good reason. As she frantically thrashed her way to the surface, gasping for air when her face broke the surface, she bumped repeatedly against the rotting corpses of animals, pieces of wood, and other waste that had been tossed into the old well.

Flailing, trying to stay afloat, she bumped her head against a rock on the side that stuck out like a small ledge— she grabbed it and clung tightly. She perched there in the bitter cold, pushing the foul-smelling floating carrion away as it bumped against her, her eyes adjusting to the darkness. She looked up and fixed her eyes on the brightness of the day above, a small circle of sky.

She shrieked, "Help me, help me! Someone please help me!"

But the walls of the well bounced her wails back to her in empty echoes.

Yoon Myoung shivered so powerfully that she lost her grip of the rock and fell back into the water. Unable to swim, she fought the water until she found the protruding rock again, and this time pulled her body halfway onto it, hugging the precarious ledge. She gazed at the patch of sunshine overhead.

After what seemed like many days, the blue sky began to cloud over and darken. Daylight was slipping away.

※

Yoon Myoung did not sleep, but she must have fallen into a sluggish stupor, because when she realized that she was hearing a voice, she knew it had been calling her for some time.

"Hello! Hello, little girl—are you still down there? Are you alive?" a voice quavered, echoing hollowly off the walls.

"Yes—yes, I am here! Please, please help me!"

"Hang on, little girl. I will drop a bucket down to you. Climb into it, and I will pull you up." The woman spoke in a hushed tone, as if to make sure no one else heard her.

Then came several minutes of quiet, and Yoon Myoung was sure that her help had vanished. But suddenly a bucket came scraping its way down the sides of the hole. It hit the water.

Yoon Myoung reached for it with one hand, unwilling to release the rock that had kept her alive all day. She missed.

"I can't reach it. I'll fall in," she whimpered.

"Then I will swing it above the water, and the bucket will find you. You can do it, little girl. Grab the bucket when it comes close to you."

The bucket did find her—it crashed on top of Yoon Myoung's head with a dull thud, but she was still too afraid to let go of the rocky ledge. "I can't do it," she cried again.

"You must! You must!" urged the woman.

"I can't!"

"If you don't, you will surely die," the woman said.

Yoon Myoung tightened her grip on the rock with one hand. With the other, she stretched as far as she could toward the rope as it swung by. Her hand closed around the rope. Pulling the bucket toward her, she struggled to maneuver her body into it while not letting go of the rock. She began to slip. Desperately, she grabbed at the rope with both hands.

"*A e go, A e go!* I'm going to die!"

"*Neon hal su-issa! Neon hal su-issa!* You can do it!"

Pulling herself up with every ounce of strength she had left, she tried again and weakly draped herself over the bucket. She sobbed, "I made it!"

The bucket twirled and swung, twirled and swung for a moment, and then Yoon Myoung could feel herself rising above the water. She crashed painfully against the side of the well many times as she was steadily pulled up.

Finally the bucket tipped over the lip of the well, and the woman gathered Yoon Myoung from the bucket into her arms and began to run. The woman was old and very small, and Yoon Myoung's feet bounced against the ground as the woman struggled to hold her up.

The woman stopped at an oxen stall and cradled Yoon Myoung. She grabbed handfuls of dry hay and rubbed it on Yoon Myoung's skin, trying to dry her off and warm her. She could not see the woman's face, but Yoon Myoung knew she must be a grandmother. Yoon Myoung shifted in the woman's arms, and the woman gently pulled her closer.

"Look at me, little girl."

Yoon Myoung gazed into the tender, watery eyes, surrounded by saggy, wrinkled skin.

"Little girl, these people want to hurt you, but it is very important that you live! Do you hear me? You must live."

Those familiar words jolted Yoon Myoung. "Do you know my mommy?"

"No, I don't. But listen to me. It's very important. You must live!"

The woman lay Yoon Myoung, still naked, on the ground and piled loose hay around her, then rose. "I must leave, but I will come back soon. Wait here."

Yoon Myoung was so tired she almost fell asleep. Several minutes later, a rustling stirred her. The old woman had returned.

"This is for you to wear," she said. She held a farmer's old gray smock in her withered hand. Cupped in her other palm was a handful of dried minnows. Yoon Myoung's eyes widened, and she snatched the treasure.

"Don't let the farmers find you. You must be gone by the time the sun comes up. Remember, little girl—you must live."

Exhausted, she gulped down the meager meal, pulled the shirt over her head, and fell into a fitful sleep.

※

Yoon Myoung sprang awake as the crow of a rooster ushered in a new day. Remembering the touch of the kind grandmother who had saved her and held her so tenderly, she arose with a heavy heart and forced herself to set out again before the village roused itself.

"I must live," she whispered to herself. "I must live."

CHAPTER 22

Taejon

Yoon Myoung's daily struggle to survive had made her senses acute. She was aware of every farmer or villager before they saw her. Her hearing was attuned to even the rustle of a grasshopper on a nearby blade of grass.

She traveled alone.

Yoon Myoung no longer tried to fool herself that she was still moving toward her home. She had lost her way, and the beginning of her journey was such a distant memory that she had no idea if her mother was toward the rising or the setting sun. She had only one goal now—not to find her mother, but simply to stay alive.

⇥⇤

As Yoon Myoung crested a mountain trail, she beheld a large city in the valley below. She gasped—then crouched to consider what to do. The city spread for miles! She wanted to turn and run—after all, each time she ventured into the vicinity of people, something terrible happened to her.

And yet a part of her was drawn to this place. She had never seen such activity! Perhaps, amid so many people, no one would notice her.

Eventually curiosity won out. She walked cautiously down the trail toward the city.

Yoon Myoung spent the morning wandering throughout the city, amazed. People were everywhere! Hundreds of bicycles weaved among ox carts piled with every imaginable ware. Yoon Myoung was occasionally bumped or shoved by the crowd, but no one seemed to notice her. As she neared the center of the city, the crowds got larger, voices became louder, and she became uneasy, wishing she hadn't entered the city at all. Everything seemed to close in around Yoon Myoung, used to the open spaces of the countryside. This was so alien to her—people everywhere, far too many of them. She felt as if she were getting swallowed up. She began to look for a way out, wanting the familiarity of the country.

A train whistled nearby, and she headed toward the sound. As she made her way through a vast, crowded, open market, she heard someone shout, "Tougee, tougee!"

But this time, the voice did not seem angry or hateful, so rather than running to hide, she stopped and searched for the source of the voice. She peeked through the throng but couldn't find who had called out for her.

Again: "Tougee!"

Then there he was, a tall, teenage boy, approaching with a grin. Other children, dirty and ragged, followed him. Yoon Myoung froze, panicked. She wanted to run, but, wary, she stood her ground. His voice and his face implied no threat.

Then he stood next to her. "You're new here, aren't you?" the tall boy asked.

Yoon Myoung nodded.

"You have a place to live?"

"No," she said.

With a smile and a nod, the boy said, "Come with us. I am the older brother of this group. I'm called Oppa."

No one had ever asked Yoon Myoung to live with them before. Even before the day of the train ride, living with her mother and her uncle and relatives in the village, she had never felt welcome. And since then, on her journey, most people just wanted her to leave. But could she trust this group? Strangers had always hurt her. She thought of the beating in the marketplace, and the shaman with her knife, and the well. Even so—these children seemed kind. She stared at this boy who called himself Oppa.

"Come on," he motioned. "We can help take care of you."

Someone to help take care of me. What would that be like? Does that mean I won't be cold or hungry again? Yoon Myoung thought.

Throwing caution aside, she replied, "Okay, I'll come."

Oppa and the others turned and walked away. Yoon Myoung scurried to keep up. Oppa looked back occasionally to make sure the little tougee girl was still following. A large bridge loomed ahead. She followed the children on a path that took them down to the river. Under the bridge, Yoon Myoung stopped dead still in utter disbelief.

Children of all ages covered the embankments, which were blanketed by clusters of makeshift shacks. Some children were digging in the debris. Others seemed to be working on their huts with branches and scrap metal. Still others were picking through one another's lice-ridden hair. Onlookers lay listlessly on mats.

Oppa motioned her to follow. As they wove through the rubble, Yoon Myoung could feel the stares.

Pointing toward a child with light hair and strange eyes, Oppa casually said, "There's another tougee."

Another girl had unusually dark skin and curly black hair. This child hung her head; Yoon Myoung could barely see her eyes.

Oppa introduced Yoon Myoung to the rest of his ragged troupe. He was their caretaker and guardian.

"Do you want to live with us? I'll take care of you too."

Yoon Myoung wasn't certain she wanted to stay with this bunch of children. Hard experience had taught her to trust no one. So without answering, she looked around at the many other groups within this large orphan camp, each of which seemed to have staked out their own territory.

"Do you know all of these people?" Yoon Myoung asked.

"Not all of them," responded Oppa. "They're not all part of my family. *This* is *my* 'family,'" he said, gesturing toward those children in the near vicinity.

There were many clusters of other "families" in this camp under the bridge, but Oppa's consisted of six or seven children.

"Okay," she said. "I'll stay." Actually, she hadn't yet

decided if she would, but she was afraid of his response if she answered any other way. Besides, she longed for companionship. Why *wouldn't* she want to be part of a family again?

That night she spent time by the fire with her new family. Oppa told ghost stories. Yoon Myoung was enraptured with his tales and the way he changed his voice and gestured with his arms during the scary parts. Then other children spoke, mostly of their adventures before coming to the bridge. The laughter the children shared over past predicaments soothed Yoon Myoung's apprehension.

The next morning, Oppa brought Yoon Myoung some clothing. He had traveled into the city and pilfered it from one of the vendors. He also produced some carrots, cucumbers, and part of a melon.

"These are for you, little sister," he smiled, handing them to her.

She felt a strange sort of happiness, and quickly went to the outer parts of this bridge village to change into her new clothes.

Later that day, with a young girl from the pack, Yoon Myoung made her way to the river to quench her thirst. As she knelt at the edge, something brushed against her leg. Startled, she jumped back—and saw a furry creature with a long, hairless tail.

"A rat!" She kicked at it, but it seemed unafraid of her, retreating no farther than necessary to avoid her foot. "Are there others?"

The girl giggled. "They're everywhere here, feeding on the garbage. Be sure to wrap cloth around your toes and fingers before going to bed or they'll nibble on them during the night."

"Is that the truth?" Yoon Myoung asked. After the storytelling from the night before, she wasn't sure what was true and what was in fun.

"Yes, it's the truth!" the girl replied. "Just remember, if you scream at them and jump up and down, they will stay away from you."

Rats or not, for the first time since leaving her mother, Yoon Myoung felt as if she'd found a home. These children all seemed like her in some strange way. She didn't feel like such a dirty tougee around them.

⥤⥢

The group's main time together was around the campfire at night. There was always much commotion around this blaze. Children came and went, sharing their plunder. The younger ones poked sticks into the fire while listening to the older one's antics of the day. Songs would break out, along with outbursts of laughter and occasionally a fight. One night, Yoon Myoung joined in the chorus of a folk song that she recognized from her mother's home. Excited to be able to contribute, she sang the last few lines solo, which the others seemed to have forgotten, and she was warmly rewarded with applause.

"Little sister, you sing like a canary," Oppa said.

"Sing some more for us," another said.

From that night on, Yoon Myoung sang for her new family every evening. It became the highlight of her day.

Yoon Myoung remembered all of those who had chased

her away, thrown rocks at her—even thrown her into pits or tied her to a waterwheel! They had tried to kill her. But she had survived. She had not died—and now she had a family. She belonged somewhere. She was valued and accepted.

She thought it odd, though, in the midst of such acceptance and mutual support, that so many of the children in Oppa's family and the other groups around them had downcast eyes and expressionless faces. She watched many of them and sensed sorrow, shame, and embarrassment.

Occasionally children from the other families would join them around the warmth of the fire. One evening, Yoon Myoung found herself drawn to a boy sitting on a rock on the other side of the fire, intently staring into the dancing flames. His face began to contort, and his head moved back and forth with the movement of the flames. His eyes glazed, fixed on the burning pit. He stood and moved closer to the fire. He leaned toward it, then pulled himself back slowly.

What is he doing? wondered Yoon Myoung.

She looked around—no one else seemed to notice him. Again he leaned toward the flames, and took a step closer. Then he swayed from side to side, never taking his gaze from the crackling fire, and inching closer and closer to it. His hands stretched in front of him till they almost touched the flames.

Without warning, he leaned forward one last time and dropped himself, face-first, into the fire.

When the boy landed in the coals, he let out a blood-curdling scream. Everyone around the fire leaped to their feet in panic, but no one did anything to help him. Young Myoung was frozen, unable to move in any direction. The boy's scant clothing was now ablaze, and the smell of burning flesh sickened Yoon Myoung.

Then Oppa came. He dragged the boy out onto the ground and began extinguishing the flames with handfuls of dirt. His clothing still smoldered, and the stench of his burnt skin was unbearable. Two boys, careful of his burns, carried the moaning boy to the river.

Yoon Myoung never saw him after that night.

⁂

One evening, nearly a month after her arrival, Oppa sauntered up to where Yoon Myoung was drawing in the dirt with a stick. Other boys followed him. Some she knew, but the rest were strangers. Oppa looked down at her and smiled. He motioned her toward the shack where she now slept with her new family of orphans. The hut was empty— the rest of the kids were warming themselves by the fire. The look on Oppa's face was different on this night, and Yoon Myoung wanted to go join the others by the fire.

In the hut, Oppa laid a mat on the ground, smoothed it out, patted it, and told her to lie on it. Yoon Myoung did as she was told. Oppa had treated her well, so she lay down on her back and stared up at Oppa, towering above her like a giant.

He slowly knelt beside her in the dirt. "Everything's going to be okay," he said and lay on top of her. She felt smothered; she had difficulty breathing.

"What are you doing, Oppa? You're too heavy!"

"Be quiet," he said. "I said it would be okay."

A few moments later, Yoon Myoung felt a horrible pain rip inside of her. It hurt so badly she was unable to move. What was happening? She looked into Oppa's face, and his expression was unlike any she had ever seen on anyone before.

He got up and left the hut without saying a word.

But even after he left, the searing pain didn't stop. Yoon Myoung didn't understand what had just happened to her, nor did she understand why. But she knew it wasn't a good thing. She curled onto her side and pulled herself into a fetal position. There, where she had just been lying, she saw blood on the mat.

Before she could get up and move, another boy entered and knelt beside her. He, too, stretched himself on top of her, and it happened all over again. One after another, the boys kept coming in, and the same horrible thing happened again and again.

By the time it was over, Yoon Myoung's silent tears had dried. No one would come to rescue her here.

◈

Yoon Myoung learned, that night, that there was a price for the clothes, food, protection, and the privilege of sitting at the fire and of lying next to the others at night to stay warm. Sometimes at night she heard girls cry out with the same screams that echoed inside her heart. She knew what was happening, and she hurt with them. Now she understood why many of the girls had such looks of desolation and shame.

Yoon Myoung felt numb. Though there were benefits to belonging to this family, this wasn't any better than what she'd had before; it was simply different.

Yoon Myoung often remembered the boy who'd dropped himself into the flames. *He was brave*, she would think. *Could I do that to myself? If I did, then I would die. I think I might like to die.*

CHAPTER 23

Summer Fever

Summer in the orphan encampment under the bridge brought sweltering heat, raw sewage in the water, and maggots and flies in the piles of garbage nearby. The air was full of mosquitoes, and much of the food the children scavenged was rotten.

Toward the end of summer, Yoon Myoung woke up one day weak, confused, and very thirsty. A wave of cramping overtook her as she lay on her mat. She cried out, but no one responded. Where was everyone?

Slowly, she raised her head and looked around. The spaces next to her were empty—the children who slept in them, gone. Crawling to the shanty's entrance, she peered out. There was only bare dirt, not even a leftover bed mat. The fire had burned down. Oppa and the rest of Yoon Myoung's family had packed up and left her behind. Where had they gone?

Despite her foggy-headed confusion, she vaguely remembered the night before. At the campfire, Oppa, who had noticed her frequent diarrhea and incessant shaking, had pushed Yoon Myoung away.

"Little sister, you stink like a rotten fish!" he had snarled at her.

"I'm sorry," Yoon Myoung replied. "I don't mean to." *Do I really smell that bad?* she wondered.

"You must have some disease. You'll make us all sick!" he scolded.

Now, feebly, Yoon Myoung scanned the surrounding area for anyone from her family. She stumbled to the riverbank, calling for Oppa, but there was no answer.

Yoon Myoung had suffered much since losing her mother: the loss of her childhood and innocence, isolation, beatings ... but the anguish that flooded her at this moment, at the shock of being left behind under this bridge, made it nearly impossible to breathe. Her heart hammered against the inside of her chest. She could no longer stand, so she sat abruptly and took several deep breaths.

Anger welled up from deep within—slowly at first, and then more rapidly it spread throughout her body.

Did they leave me because I have a disease? How could they do that? They are my family. Oppa told me that!

The other orphan groups remained in this camp under the bridge, but her family had moved on ... without her. Her absence wouldn't change a thing for those who remained in Oppa's family. She was less than a ripple on the river to them. But if they returned to this bridge, she wouldn't be there.

"I'll show them!" Yoon Myoung shook with rage. "I hate them! I hate, hate, hate them!"

Staggering up the embankment, she paused for one last look toward the camp. *This is not my family!* She turned and walked away.

Yoon Myoung had seen where the train tracks cut through this city as she'd wandered that first day, and she had passed the train station. She entered a dark, damp alley that she knew would take her there. She walked beside a shallow ditch, cluttered with debris and raw sewage. Unexpected cries startled her out of her daze, and she crouched and listened intently, searching for the source. Peering into the slimy gutter, she spotted movement. There, wrapped in only a few rags, slumped in the muck, was a small child who couldn't have been more than three years old. Yoon Myoung put one hand under the little girl's legs and the other around her waist and lifted her out of the garbage. The child's fingers clung tightly around Yoon Myoung's neck.

Rocking the toddler back and forth, she heard herself whisper, "Don't cry. Don't cry. It's okay. It's okay."

But the tearless squalling continued.

"I'll find us some food. Don't cry, little girl."

She stripped the girl and hoisted the light bundle onto her back. Tying the child to her back with the rags, she carried her to the market. Still sick herself, Yoon Myoung felt groggy, weak, and dizzy, but she was driven by a sense of urgency to quiet the baby. She waited along the edge of the market, and when an opportunity arose, she snatched a handful of cucumbers and started to run. But she made it only a few steps when she was jerked off her feet. The toddler she carried tumbled from her back and landed on the hard ground. Her legs still swinging in the air, Yoon Myoung twisted around and saw the wrinkled, scowling face of a livid farmer who held her up by her knotted, dirty hair.

"It's you, dirty tougee! I caught you this time!" he bellowed.

The baby was shrieking. Yoon Myoung lunged to escape, but the old man's fingers were so entangled in her hair, she couldn't budge. Sickness had drained her, and she was no match for this angry farmer.

He shouted to the nearby merchants and farmers, "It's the dirty tougee again!"

"She's a pest. We need to get rid of her," hissed another man.

"She's the child of a pig," said the first.

Yoon Myoung tried to bat away the farmer's arm, but she was too weak and slow.

"Look—they've got the summer fever!" cried one of the men.

"Get rid of them before they give it to us!"

"Let's take them to the building!"

Yoon Myoung knew what that meant. The "building" was a bombed building, now long abandoned and left as a breeding ground for the huge rats that lived along the river.

As they were being dragged to the building, Yoon Myoung moaned, "Please, no. Please, no. Not the building. Please don't take me there."

The tiny girl whimpered but was too weak to fight those who dragged her.

A crowd of villagers followed curiously along.

"Stop! Just let them go!" she heard someone holler.

Others shouted, "No! They're thieves!"

Soon the building came into view. A concrete wall, too high for a child to climb, enclosed it. Her hands were grabbed by one farmer, her feet by another, and they swung her back and forth in widening arcs. Yoon Myoung went limp just before they let go, tossing her over the wall as if she were a bag of rice. She landed with a crash on the other side, in a burst of intense pain. But she had no time to feel sorry for herself. She desperately groped the concrete floor, searching for the toddler, whose whimpers had ceased.

She soon found the child, bloodied and still. Yoon Myoung clung to the little body, rocking her back and forth, back and forth. She sang a quiet song and rocked. The little girl hung limply in Yoon Myoung's arms. Her chest never moved with breath.

Yoon Myoung felt terribly sick. Her mouth felt as dry as the hay she slept on at night. Her body shook with fever. Her breaths came rapidly. She knew that she needed to stay awake. The rats would appear soon, and she had nothing with which to cover and protect her feet and hands. She still clutched the lifeless girl in her arms.

"Stay awake," she said aloud to herself. "Yoon Myoung, you must stay awake."

Then she saw the first rat sticking its nose out of the shadows. Slowly it emerged. More rats appeared, noses twitching and whiskers wiggling, as they sniffed their way along the concrete. Their black, beady eyes were intent. Yoon Myoung did the only thing she knew to do.

Remembering the advice of the girl under the bridge, mustering all of her strength, she screamed as long and loudly as she could. She screamed ... and screamed ... and screamed ...

Sometime later, Yoon Myoung found herself rousing groggily from unconsciousness. Nearby, the rats swarmed over the body of the little girl Yoon Myoung had tried so desperately to protect. There was blood, too, on her own stinging fingers. She looked around, still mostly in a fog, hoping to see someone or something that might rescue her. But it was too hard to hold up her head. She laid it down one more time ...

PART 3

CHAPTER 24

She Is Mine!

It had been a long, strenuous day. Taking care of destitute babies with such pressing needs was exhausting work. Sweden and home seemed a lifetime away. But in living out her convictions by caring for others, the missionary nurse felt incredibly fulfilled.

The blue-eyed, fair-skinned blonde had come to South Korea to care for infants left to die on the streets, acting on what had long been her passion. She was dedicated to finding babies, bringing them back to health, and getting them into orphanages. But she found an even greater challenge than she had expected: The needs of the impoverished were so great in post-war Korea that she had taught herself to mentally put on blinders to other children, even toddlers, to remain single-minded and devoted to the orphaned infants.

All day she tended the babies at her medical clinic. Once a child was healthy, she would pack up a few meager supplies and transport the infant through the dirt streets of Daejeon to an orphanage across town. This day, she carried a six month old, now strong enough to go to the orphanage.

She grew so attached to each child during their time at the clinic that it was difficult for her to discharge them, but she reminded herself that she had been trained for the sick. She said her good-byes to this little one, planted a kiss on his cheek, handed him to the smiling attendant at the orphanage, and quickly left, fighting her emotions.

This night something drew her back along a different route to her clinic, through a road called Garbage Lane, which cut through Daejeon's landfill. Many people lived there and called it home. Bedraggled children trailed behind her, begging for food. Many suffered from sores, disease, and war injuries. Wanting to help them, and yet needing to get home before dusk, she put on her "blinders" and hurried along the refuse-lined paths.

Hearing a whimper, she hesitated, listening carefully. Why am I stopping? she wondered. There were so many needy ones, and she couldn't possibly help them all.

Yet she felt compelled to investigate. She heard the whimper again, and following the sound, she found a little girl lying unconscious in a heap of garbage.

Her blinders fell away.

"Oh, dear God," she said aloud. "How did she end up here?"

Kneeling beside the child, she saw immediately that this little one was near death. Her skin sagged from dehydration and she had many open sores, many of them no doubt inflicted by the rats the woman could hear scurrying in the growing darkness. Filth and dried blood caked the girl's body.

"Little girl, little girl, wake up," she said tenderly.

Nothing happened, so she said, more loudly this time, "Wake up, little girl, wake up!"

Leaning over the child, she gently shook her shoulder. Eyelashes fluttered, and the girl's eyes slowly opened ...

※

Yoon Myoung thought she was looking into the face of some sort of spirit: yellow hair shimmering like sunshine, captivating blue eyes overflowing with tender compassion. Had she died? No ... her aches and pains assured her that she was very much alive.

Confused, Yoon Myoung whispered, "Am I in paradise?"

"No, little girl, you're not in paradise," the yellow-haired spirit answered.

※

The nurse shook her head. We have too many babies already at the clinic, she argued with herself. What can I do with this child? She's too old anyway, and besides, she's so far gone that I doubt I can do anything to help her. I need to leave her here.

Slowly, the woman rose to her feet, wondering why she had even come this way to begin with. She lingered just a moment over the dying child, wishing she could work miracles, and then, with a heavy sigh, turned her back and began to walk away. She had taken only a few steps when, to her amazement, she found herself unable to move. Her legs suddenly felt as if they had been buried in concrete.

Why can't I move? What's wrong?

She concentrated on trying to move her legs against the force that held her, to take a step, to continue on her way

*back to the clinic. And then she heard a voice. It wasn't a
sensation, or a feeling, or a thought. It was an audible voice
in her native Swedish, a language she hadn't heard since
leaving her homeland.*

"She ... is ... mine!"

*Startled, still unable to move, the nurse looked around
her for the Swede who had just spoken. No one was there.
She was alone in the garbage heap.*

And that's when she knew who had spoken to her.

*Shaken and in awe, she had no choice but to take the tou-
gee child with her. And having made that choice, she found
that her legs lightened, and she was able to move toward
the little girl. She scooped her from the debris and gingerly
carried her to the clinic.*

⤚⤙

When the yellow-haired woman had stood and begun to
walk away, Yoon Myoung had watched from her pile of
garbage, too sick to care. Then she rolled onto her side to
watch the sun disappear back into the earth. And suddenly
she wondered: She had lost consciousness in the building
full of rats, where the cruel men had thrown her. Now she
seemed to be out in the landfill, on a pile of garbage. How
had she gotten here?

She was startled when she felt a hand gently brushing
her shoulder, then felt herself being lifted into the woman's
arms.

"Don't worry, little girl. I will make you better. There is
nothing to be afraid of anymore."

Yoon Myoung groaned in pain. The woman's words

meant nothing to her. People might promise Yoon Myoung
good things, but there was always pain. She drifted into a
deep sleep.

⊱⊰

Over the next few days, Yoon Myoung received liquids
through a tube into her arm, and medicine to treat the
summer fever. Soon she was able to eat three meals each
day—and she didn't even have to scavenge for it! She had
no words for this place, or even for the kind nurses who
took great care in dealing with her animal bites, infections,
and the layers of filth baked into her skin. She spent several
days in bed before she was strong enough to satisfy her
curiosity by venturing around the clinic compound. Cautiously, she crept along the immaculate open-air hallways
that lined the courtyard of the clinic. She saw tiny hands
and feet poking out of infant baskets resting on tables—
twelve bassinets in each very clean room.

Korean nurses in crisp white uniforms monitored the
swaddled infants. Each room was very bright because of
sunlight that entered through square "openings" in the
walls. She could look through the squares and see the
world outside, but once when she reached for the opening, her hand bumped against something, and it "pinged"
against her nails. She leaned closer to examine the square
and was surprised by her own shadowy reflection. It was
made of something as transparent and reflective as water—
and that let in the light. Everything in the clinic seemed to
sparkle because of the summer sun that entered the room
through these squares.

A magical flower garden nestled between the clinic and the angel nurse's home. Yoon Myoung had never seen such beauty all in one place. Walking among the blossoms reminded her of the springtime wildflowers in the countryside. Despite their busyness, despite the cooing and crying of babies, these caregivers, including her rescuer, would always stop to smile and let Yoon Myoung know she was noticed.

A cement wall crowned with glass shards encircled the clinic, making Yoon Myoung feel protected and secure for the first time since she had left her village two years ago. Sleep came easily now. She felt as if she really must be in paradise. She hoped that she could live inside this safe haven forever.

CHAPTER 25

Mi Yun

One morning, Yoon Myoung rolled out of her quilt, washed her face beneath the outside water spigot, brushed her teeth with a salted finger, and ate her barley cereal. As she eagerly headed outside to the flower garden, a nurse with a white cap perched on her head and carrying a cloth bag approached.

"Would you like to go for a walk?" she asked Yoon Myoung.

Yoon Myoung reluctantly followed the woman through the gate—her first time to leave this sanctuary since her arrival.

The nurse looked down at Yoon Myoung and announced cheerily, "I'm taking you to an orphanage. There are many children your age there. This is going to be so nice for you. You will really enjoy living there."

But Yoon Myoung had heard about an orphanage from children under the bridge. They described it like a jail, vowing that they would rather live on the streets than in an orphanage.

Her heart beat faster. *Why was she being taken there? They wouldn't take me to a place worse than the streets, would they? No, the other children must be wrong. They must not really know what an orphanage is like.*

But those attempts to reassure herself did not slow the wild beating of her heart. Yoon Myoung turned to steal one last look at the clinic that had become her home. She loved this place.

People moved out of the way for this woman in uniform. She strode quickly. Yoon Myoung needed to run every few steps to keep up. Why were grown-ups always rushing?

It seemed that their journey took many hours, but eventually they stopped in front of a huge, light-green, metal entryway. High concrete walls surrounded the orphanage compound, topped with broken bottles, just like at her clinic "home." Yoon Myoung reassured herself that, just like at the clinic, bad people couldn't get in.

The nurse clanged on an iron knocker. Immediately, a cut-out door in the gate creaked open. After they entered, the nurse instructed Yoon Myoung to stand by the door and wait. Then she marched to a gray cement-block building in the center of the grounds.

The compound was large—larger than the children's village under the bridge—and much was happening. Women and older girls swept the dirt floors, while others carried babies, and still others were hanging clothing on clotheslines. A group of boys plucking weeds and small stones from a vegetable garden stopped their work for a moment and stared at Yoon Myoung.

After several minutes, the nurse and an older Korean woman emerged from the building and approached Yoon Myoung, who immediately fixed her eyes on the ground. Her heart began to pound anxiously. Then she felt someone patting her on the head—the older woman. Keeping her head down, Yoon Myoung peered up wide-eyed.

The nurse from the clinic knelt in front of Yoon Myoung. "This kind lady runs this orphanage. You will need to listen to her and follow her instructions at all times. You will call her *Halmoni*, Grandmother. She is very busy, and there are many children who live here, and many others who want to live here. It is a privilege to live here, an honor. You need to be a good girl."

The nurse turned to leave. Oh, how Yoon Myoung wanted to chase after her and beg to be taken back to the clinic. But with those parting words fresh in her mind, she didn't move. She knew she mustn't protest.

"Follow me, child!" said Halmoni.

Yoon Myoung obediently shadowed Halmoni to a bleak L-shaped building which had been newly built to house the children who had been orphaned by the war. She strode up the landing and entered the first open doorway of the long hallway. Down this hallway were many doors, each opening to a dormitory-type room. Halmoni put Yoon Myoung's cloth bag on the floor.

"This will be your space," announced Halmoni, gesturing toward the nearest corner. "You will share this room with seven other girls. This building is for girls. The building next door is for the boys." She began to walk again. "Come with me."

Stepping outside, Halmoni pointed back to the big building in the center of the compound. "I live over there."

She turned toward Yoon Myoung and scrutinized her. "You will get up early, do your chores, line up with the other children in the courtyard to do your morning exercises, and listen carefully to all my instructions. Do you understand what I'm saying?"

Yoon Myoung nodded.

"Very good. You may go back to your room now and wait there for the other girls to come back from school. They will be here soon."

Yoon Myoung befuddled, retreated to her space in the corner of the sleeping quarters and waited. Squatting on the papered floor, she surveyed the room. Hooks lined the white walls, each labeled with words Yoon Myoung could not read. She would learn later that every girl living in the room had her own hook on which to hang her school uniform. The room was stark except for the sliding doors of the bedding closet.

Yoon Myoung needed to use the toilet. Cautiously, she tiptoed to the porch and scanned the courtyard until she located the outhouse. She waited until there was no one around to see her, then scurried toward the wooden shack. Opening the flimsy wooden door and stepping onto the two planks, one positioned for each foot, she resisted the urge to gag at the stench. Horseflies swarmed all around. She balanced carefully on these planks, fearful of falling through the hole into the large barrel underneath. Suddenly she heard a commotion outside. Peeking out of the door, she spotted school children flocking through the front gate. Frightened of what they might do or say if they saw her, she stayed in the outhouse.

But one of the girls pulled open the outhouse door and then stopped, looking at Yoon Myoung strangely. Realizing that she couldn't remain there, Yoon Myoung braced herself for what lay ahead and shuffled out into the now-crowded courtyard. Most of the girls were busy laughing and talking among themselves. Some greeted her, while others simply walked on to their rooms without a word or smile. The girls' friendly chatter soothed her, and her fear began to subside.

A bell clanged in the courtyard. The girls quickly exited the dorm and formed a line along the porch. Yoon Myoung noticed the boys piling out from their building and lining up as well.

"I'm so hungry," said one of the girls.

"Me too!" chimed many all at once.

Thinking that they must be gathering for a meal, Yoon Myoung lined up as well. Halmoni emerged from her building, flanked by two men she later learned were Halmoni's sons. As the trio stood aside, the two men looked carefully at the children marching past them into the dining hall. They frightened Yoon Myoung, and she kept her head down as she walked by.

A bowl of yellow mush with some sort of greens ladled on top was placed before her. Yoon Myoung was just starting to reach for the food when she realized that no one else was moving. She waited and observed. Halmoni, in a booming voice, told the children to bow their heads. They all did, including Yoon Myoung, and then Halmoni spoke of a God. After Halmoni stopped talking, loud chatter broke out among the orphans, along with the sound of spoons clanging against metal bowls as the children devoured their food. It was different from the clinic food, but Yoon Myoung swallowed it gratefully.

After they finished and cleaned up, some girls played hopscotch in the courtyard while boys played a game they called "kick the can." Yoon Myoung chose to sit on the porch of the girl's dorm and watch from a distance.

When the bell rang again, the children scurried into their rooms, pulled out their bedrolls, and spread them on the floor. They went back outside to scrub at a wash station. One child would operate the handle, pulling it up and pushing down, until water began to pour out of the pump's spigot. The others stood in line to scrub their faces and teeth before heading back inside to their bedding.

For the first time since she had left her mama, Yoon Myoung was reminded of her great-grandparents and the strictness and structure of her home. She understood the reason for the nurse's rigid order, "You will need to listen to Halmoni and follow her instructions at all times."

The next morning, the bell startled Yoon Myoung out of her sleep, and the morning routine began. After storing their bedrolls and changing into school or work clothes, the orphans formed straight rows in the courtyard like little soldiers. The boys were in one section, the girls in another. With Halmoni bellowing orders on a megaphone, the children started morning calisthenics in unison. Yoon Myoung tried desperately to copy what they were doing but became quickly exhausted. She crumpled onto the ground. Halmoni immediately marched over to her and ordered her to rise. Yoon Myoung weakly stood and forced herself to join in. Fortunately, the exercises were soon over. The children stood at rigid attention.

"We have another day ahead of us. There is much you must do to keep this orphanage looking clean and nice. I expect each of you to do your part.

"Remember why you are here. Some of you are here because you were orphaned. Some of you are here because you were not wanted by your families. All of you are here because you needed a place to live and someone to take care of you. Now you have that. And if you want to stay here, you must be respectful, obedient, and you must stay out of trouble. I expect you to help one another. If you cannot do as you are told, you will be punished. This is a very good place, and you are very fortunate to live here. There are many orphanages in Korea, but the one you live in is the best."

Then Halmoni disappeared into the big building, and a breakfast bell rang.

Yoon Myoung would soon discover that every morning in the orphanage began with the same lecture.

As the children lay on their quilts that evening, one of the girls asked, "Young sister, what is your name?"

"I don't have a name," replied Yoon Myoung.

The girl giggled, "Everyone has a name. My name is Mi Cha."

Yoon Myoung strained to remember when she had lived with her mother. She must have had a name. But it had been too long, and she had been called so many other names since then. She could not remember what her mama had called her.

Tougee. Tougee is my name, thought Yoon Myoung. But this was a name she didn't want to keep.

Her dreams that night were especially clear, filled with images of her mama and life from several years earlier, but Yoon Myoung awakened with no answers about her name. Distracted by her thoughts about her name, she was barely able to roll up her bedding.

Mi Cha moved over to help her. "Halmoni told me that I should show you around and give you chores to do. She wants me to be your older sister and teach you things here."

Yoon Myoung looked up into Mi Cha's kind face. She longed for such a sister. Then, remembering Oppa, she shuddered and remained silent.

After breakfast, Mi Cha taught her the morning exercises. Then Mi Cha led her to the front door of Halmoni's building and softly knocked. Halmoni opened the door, dismissed Mi Cha, and motioned Yoon Myoung in to sit before a low table in the corner of the big room. Halmoni circled behind the desk and sat down cross-legged before a kneeling Yoon Myoung.

"Little girl, do you know your name?"

"No." Hanging her head in shame, she added, "I am a tougee."

Halmoni flushed and gently contradicted the child. "No, you are not a tougee! You must never say that word again. We need to give you a name."

Yoon Myoung was quiet. A name? A real name? What

would it be? Did that mean that she wasn't a tougee anymore?

Halmoni knelt next to Yoon Myoung and put her wrinkled hand on Yoon Myoung's shoulder. With her other hand, she tilted the orphan's chin up and thoughtfully appraised her.

"Let me see … you were rescued for a reason. I think you are like a Mi Yun. We will call you that."

"A Mi Yun? What's a Mi Yun?" a bewildered Yoon Myoung wondered aloud.

"Mi Yun means 'Beautiful Dawn.'"

No one since her mama had called her beautiful. Yoon Myoung repeated the name aloud—"Mi Yun. Mi Yun. Mi Yun." She loved the way the words rolled off her tongue. She smiled.

Yoon Myoung bounded back to the dormitory. Patting the arm of the first girl she found, she announced, "My name is Mi Yun! Halmoni says my name is Mi Yun."

The other girl simply replied, "Hello, Mi Yun."

The rest of that day Yoon Myoung softly recited her new name, over and over. No longer was she a tougee. She was a Mi Yun!

CHAPTER 26

Diaper Duty

"Mi Yun, come with me and see the work we have to do today," said Mi Cha. "We have much to do, so we will be gone most of the day. Here is your lunch for later on."

She offered Mi Yun a cloth pouch that held a small barley ball and some greens. Enthralled at the sound of her new name, Mi Yun ignored her discomfort at the thought of leaving the safety of the orphanage for the day. She trusted Mi Cha and knew that she would be looking after her. Mi Cha motioned for Mi Yun to follow her, along with three others.

They made their way to the back door of an enormous storage building at the far end of the compound. A sweet, acrid odor hit Mi Yun with force.

"Phew! What's that?" she asked, scrunching up her nose.

Mi Cha simply smiled and picked up by its attached cloth straps one of several empty bamboo baskets lined up along the wall. Mi Cha placed the basket over Mi Yun's narrow shoulders and tied it tightly in front with another cloth strap. The basket was light; Mi Yun barely noticed its weight. But then Mi Cha motioned Mi Yun toward a large wooden barrel piled high with soiled diapers. Scooping out a handful of the foul rags, the older sister wrung them out and placed them into Mi Yun's basket. After the basket was filled—and much heavier, so that Mi Yun had to spread her legs wider and carefully balance its weight—she stood patiently while Mi Cha and the other three girls helped one another put on and fill their baskets. When all the dirty diapers had been divided among them, one of the girls handed Mi Yun a wide wooden board. Each of the girls carried one.

The pungent smell swirled around her head as she followed the other girls out the front gate. The load was also becoming heavy, and the sun beat on her mercilessly. But Mi Yun was excited to escape the confines of the orphanage, and she hurried to keep up.

An old truck sped suddenly past, forcing the girls to the edge of the shallow open gutter alongside the road. Mi Yun's eyes itched from the dirt stirred by the speeding truck. Seeing the muddy gutter, filled with debris and vermin, Mi Yun remembered the baby she had found in just such a place and tried to rescue. She remembered, with a chill, being thrown into that rat-infested building ... the rats ... the blood ... the little girl?

Mi Yun hastily pushed the thoughts away. She despised these memories. They changed nothing.

After trudging for nearly an hour along the road, the girls arrived at a rocky riverbank where the flow of water was suitable for washing. Mi Yun wearily plopped down on

a rock at the river's edge. Her back ached from the heavy
load. She was already tired, and their work was just beginning. She watched the others squat at the river's edge and
loosen the baskets from their backs, one strap at a time. Mi
Cha helped Mi Yun get free from her basket and its straps.

They emptied their baskets. When all the dirty diapers were piled high on the rocks, the girls squatted with
their feet in the river and swirled the soiled cloths in the
stream one at a time. Then, placing them against a flat
rock, they scrubbed each diaper with a bar of lard soap.
Now they used the wooden paddles they had brought—
they pounded the diaper with it, rinsing and rubbing again
until it smelled clean.

Other women washed their clothes along the river as
well, and the women eyed this group of orphans territori-
ally. The girls stayed downstream from them.

Mi Yun enjoyed the sense of sisterhood she felt with
this group of girls, even though the work was tiring. To
make their time more pleasurable, the girls sang. Although
Mi Yun didn't know the words, she found herself humming along with them.

After many long hours, the laundered diapers were
tossed again into the baskets for the uphill trek back to the
orphanage. Exhausted, Mi Yun pressed on regardless. *At
least when I get back*, she thought, *the hard work is done.*

But when they reached the orphanage at last, Mi Yun
discovered that her work wasn't finished after all. Instead of
returning to the storage building with the baskets, Mi Yun
followed the girls to a clothesline at the edge of the courtyard. They pulled each diaper out of the basket, shook it,

and standing on tiptoe, hung it on the line to dry. When all the washed rags had been hung, Mi Yun stumbled back to her building and fell asleep on the porch.

The clanging dinner bell stirred her awake for her next meal.

The girls' last chore before bedtime was retrieving the dry diapers from the clothesline and folding them for the next day's use.

Diaper detail at Halmoni's orphanage had officially begun for Mi Yun—six days a week. On Sundays, they rested. But Monday always brought double the amount of work.

⇥⇤

One day as they walked back through the iron gate of the orphanage, heading for the clotheslines, Mi Yun and her fellow workers saw a handful of girls and boys peeking through the cracks in the wooden door along the side of the storage house. Almost noiselessly, they snickered and whispered among themselves.

One little girl turned away from the storage house. Mi Yun and the little girl locked eyes for just a moment, and Mi Yun saw horror and pain in the little girl's eyes. The little girl hurried away, tears in her eyes. What had caused this unhappiness? Mi Yun stepped closer to try to see into the building.

But Mi Cha pulled her away roughly. "Stay away from this building on market days, Mi Yun!" she warned. "There is only trouble waiting for you there."

Mi Yun followed Mi Cha to the clotheslines.

In the days following, Mi Yun listened intently and learned much about the dark side of life at the orphanage. Once a week, Halmoni traveled into town to go to the market. Her sons were left in charge of the compound on that day. With their mother gone for several hours, they would take the older girls into the storage building. Mi Yun understood. On those days, Mi Yun would not go back to her dormitory porch. Instead she hid, by herself, behind the putrid odor of the outhouse. She remained untouched.

As the evenings became colder, Mi Yun was relieved and grateful that this winter she would not have to struggle for survival in a foxhole covered by snow. Even so, recalling that self-sufficient life created a longing in her. She remembered the independence of roaming the countryside without rules. She missed the feeling of freedom she had loved about that time in her life.

Then she remembered other things: the horrors of abuse, the realities of suffering. *Rules are better than rejection, loneliness, hunger, and pain,* she thought.

❧

When the short summer break ended, most of the children returned to school. Mi Yun continued her diaper duty with the orphanage workers while her friends went back to their studies. Since their school year began in April, and Mi Yun had joined the orphanage sometime after that, she would have to wait until the following April to begin attending school—if she had the opportunity to attend at all. It saddened her that her "sisters" were gone so much of the day. But Halmoni gave Mi Yun a new task: helping with the many infants and toddlers in the afternoons. Cradling the babies and diapering and feeding them became her favorite part of the day.

As winter approached, the temperatures dropped. Mi Yun began to dread laundering the diapers: the dark, cold early morning haul to the river and scrubbing the diapers in the cold water and frigid, dry, winter air, which left her hands cracked and raw. Mi Yun often had to use her wooden paddle to break the ice layer that covered the river.

But at the end of each dreary day, Mi Yun dashed to her reward: the babies, who warmed her chilled body as she gently rocked and sang to them.

At night before bed, Mi Yun huddled closely with the other girls around the potbelly stove in the common room, where she listened to their schoolgirl chatter, telling stories from the day. When Mi Cha stood, the younger girls knew it was time to follow her to the sleeping room where they nestled together to keep warm for the night. Secure in their body warmth and lulled to sleep by their whisperings, Mi Yun slept in peace.

CHAPTER 27

What a Friend

Mi Yun always looked forward to suppertime in the dining hall. Most nights, their entire meal was a bowl of corn mush and greens. Sometimes, Halmoni would bring her own large bowl of rice and barley into the dining hall and empty it into the big container that held the orphans' mixture of mush. It was Halmoni's way of showing kindness and compassion. Even though she was strict, Mi Yun knew that Halmoni cared deeply for the orphans.

After the evening meal, the children would remain in the dining room to complete their homework. Halmoni and her workers walked among the children, making sure they stayed on task. Giggling, bickering, or any lack of attention would bring a thump on the head or knuckles with the bamboo stick Halmoni carried. As dusk fell, small, white, ceramic jars of oil, each with a wick on top, were placed on the tables, providing just enough light for four or five orphans to crowd around and finish their homework. When the oil lamps' meager light could no longer cut through the growing darkness in the room, the leaders would enter, each carrying a lantern, and the children were led off to bed.

Although tired by the end of the day, Mi Yun found peace in being surrounded by the others. There were a few other younger girls Mi Yun's age in the orphanage who also didn't go to school, and homework hour was their time to play. Mi Yun's favorite game was played with several very long, thick rubber bands. Two girls stretched one of the rubber bands and held it flat along the ground. Two more girls stretched a second band across the ground parallel to the first, and two more girls a third. Those remaining hopped, skipped, and jumped over and between the rubber bands while softly singing a rhyme.

Later, in her room, Mi Yun would lie down between two girls, tucked in with the sense of protection and security that came from being close to others.

⤛⤜

One day in the middle of winter, Mi Yun returned to the orphanage from her daily trip to the river to find American soldiers in the courtyard, building a snowman for the orphans. When the soldiers disappeared into the dining room, Mi Yun began to hurry off to the babies—but instead, she was told to run to her room and change into her clean outfit, and be quick about it. Mi Yun worried. This had never happened before—what did it mean?

When the bell clanged, the children assembled in the snow-covered courtyard. Halmoni opened the door, and the children filed quietly into the large dining room, where they found the soldiers waiting calmly in the corner. But when the food was brought out, delighted gasps filled the room. Today's supper was thick barley, scrumptious vegetables, hot soup! It was the best thing Mi Yun had ever tasted! As she savored her meal, she stole a glance at the men in uniform. Beside them was a small tree draped with colored paper chains and topped with a wooden star.

What a strange thing these foreigners have brought to this orphanage! Mi Yun thought.

After the dishes were collected and the children were all sitting quietly on the floor facing the white soldiers, the men started singing songs. Mi Yun recognized the sound of a few words, even though she did not know what they meant, and knew that this was English, the language she had heard other white soldiers speak during her wanderings. The sound of their voices was strong and low, like the noise of thunder on a spring day. Mi Yun listened intently. One of the soldiers caught her looking at him and winked at her. She quickly looked away in embarrassment. When she snuck another peek at him, he winked again. Her heart jumped, and she blushed.

One of the soldiers dragged out one of several large, green cloth bags that were lined up under the strange tree. With a big smile, he loosened the drawstring of the bag, reached inside, and pulled out paper sacks. He handed them to the other soldiers standing nearby. Although they could barely contain their excitement, the children sat, hands folded politely in their laps, as the soldiers passed out these treasures, one to each child.

"Children, wait until all the bags have been distributed before opening yours," Halmoni said.

Will I get one? Will they know me too? Mi Yun squirmed where she sat. She watched while the bags were handed out. Finally the winking soldier held a brown sack out to her. Grinning, he spoke to her in words she did not understand—but she knew one thing: He was giving one of the wonderful bags to her.

Mi Yun gently shook her bag and crinkled its paper. *What's inside?* When she was sure that Halmoni wasn't watching, she tore open a small hole, even though she was told to wait. But the hole was too small—she still couldn't see what was inside.

As the last child received his gift, Halmoni called, "You are only allowed to eat one piece of the candy tonight. Only one!"

Mi Yun's bag contained a small toy along with three hard candies: red, green, and yellow.

"Which one should I choose?" Mi Yun said out loud.

After thoughtfully inspecting each piece, she settled on the red one. She carefully removed the crinkly, shiny outer wrapping and placed it in her pocket. Then she popped the candy into her mouth. Her lips puckered with the sweetness. She savored each moment as it dissolved on her tongue. Then it was gone.

The men wandered throughout the crowd of children, patting them on their heads or backs and shaking their hands. Some of the men lifted the younger children high into the air, eliciting giggles and occasionally a frantic scream.

Mi Yun was sad when it was time for the soldiers to say good-bye. These men were so kind, and this celebration had been so full of laughter. Halmoni led the workers and children in a bow of thanks to the soldiers, and they all waved as their truck pulled away.

After the GIs had disappeared, Halmoni ordered the orphans back into the dining hall, where to Mi Yun's surprise and heartache, Halmoni collected the remaining candies and all the toys. Each of the children resignedly placed their treats in one large basket and their toys in another. Some of the youngest children cried. They all silently watched as Halmoni took the baskets into the storage room. Emerging a moment later, she locked the door behind her.

Mi Cha leaned close and whispered, "Halmoni will save them for the future, in case of lack."

❈

Awakening one night to the chill of a winter draft, Mi Yun rolled over to reach for the warmth of those who lay next to her. Instead she felt a cold absence—an empty space! The girl who slept next to her was missing.

Although it wasn't common for the girls, sometimes the boys fled the security and warmth of the orphanage for the call of the street. To them, freedom was more important than safety. The unyielding discipline for breaking the rules was severe. A bamboo stick across the back of the legs or on the head or hands kept them all in check.

The girl who was missing was one of those regularly taken by Halmoni's sons to the storage house on market days. Mi Yun understood her temptation to run.

❈

On Sundays, Mi Yun would rise in the morning and slip into her nicer dress. On this day, the children were permitted to go straight to breakfast, with no exercises first! After the morning meal, they would march through the courtyard, out the front gate, and up the hill to the Presbyterian church. The orphans would sit cross-legged on the floor in the back of the church.

At her first church service, Mi Yun had sat wide-eyed, taking in all that was going on around her. It had started with enthusiastic singing, and many of the children had joined in, clapping and lifting their hands to the music. Halmoni hadn't stopped them, and in fact, like some of the other adults, she had sung with her eyes closed, tears flowing down her cheeks. Mi Yun reveled in this new experience. It gave her another taste of belonging.

After much singing, a very short man climbed the stairs that led to the stage and stood, nearly hidden behind a mammoth wooden podium. Mi Yun could barely see his head—so she was startled by his booming voice. How could such a loud voice come from such a little man? He opened a big book on the stand and bellowed, thrusting his arms into the air as if batting away pesky flies. The gathering lasted several hours.

Sunday after Sunday, the children would file into this church. Week after week, Mi Yun heard the words:
Love.
God.
Everlasting Life.
Jesus.

Questions began to form in Mi Yun's mind. *Who is this God? What is love? Why did God give away his son?*

Since there was no one to answer her questions, she came to her own conclusions. *This God loves the world, but I am not part of this world. I am a mistake. I am a tougee. He can't love me because I don't belong to him, or to anyone.*

Though she couldn't read the hymnals, Mi Yun soon memorized the lyrics. She loved singing the melodies with all of her might. "Amazing Grace," "Great Is Thy Faithfulness," "What a Friend We Have in Jesus." That last one was one of her favorites. It always caused her to think . . .

"What a friend we have in Jesus . . . "

Jesus is my friend? Really? Where is he? I want a friend.

"Oh, what needless pain we bear,
"All because we do not carry
"Everything to God in prayer."

I can take everything to him? Can I take the diaper basket to Jesus? I don't want to carry it anymore.

"Who will all our sorrows share?"

I'm sad. The girl who ran away was sad, too. I miss her.

"Are we weak and heavy-laden,
"Cumbered with a load of care?"

Yes, I'm weak! I don't like this burden of diapers every day. How do I take the loads of heavy diapers to Jesus, and will he carry them for me?

"Do thy friends despise, forsake thee?"

They still call me tougee when Halmoni isn't listening.

⊱⊰

After each service, a wide variety of foods that were never offered at the orphanage were laid out on low tables along the walls of the building. Although the children were allowed to sit with the church members and eat these foods, Halmoni restricted their portions. After the meal, the orphans played together in the church courtyard. This was the best day of the week!

CHAPTER 28

Starting School

The winter snow of 1962 melted away. The school year finished at the end of February, and the children were released for their break. As the biting March winds gave way to the breath of April, Halmoni surprised Mi Yun. "You will be starting school with the other children, Mi Yun," she announced.

Will I like going to school? She had heard the other girls of the orphanage talk about school, and some of the stories they told didn't sound like fun. And besides, she enjoyed the evening playtime with the young girls while the older ones did their homework.

But she would no longer have to do diaper duty!

For the first day of school, Mi Yun was given a tan cotton blouse and navy-blue skirt. Her stomach fluttered wildly as she dressed in this new uniform. She pranced among the other orphanage children as they marched out of the gate, onto the dirt road, and wound their way through the neighborhood to a huge elementary school.

To Mi Yun's disappointment, school was very much like the orphanage. Upon their arrival, the children lined up in rows in the courtyard of the school. A strict female voice boomed through a loudspeaker, giving almost the same talk as Halmoni's daily lecture.

"We have another day of school ahead of us. There is much work and learning for you to do. I expect each of you to do your best. If you want to stay in school, you must be obedient and respectful and follow the rules. If you cannot fit in here, you will be punished. This school is a very nice school. Many children are not privileged to attend school. Know that you are very fortunate to be able to learn here."

When, after the lecture, a male teacher began to call out exercise drills, Mi Yun's heart sank. After exercises, the children were excused to their classrooms. When she entered her classroom, the teacher, a man, directed Mi Yun to a chair in the front of the room. Excited to sit at the front, Mi Yun waited expectantly for what would happen next. She soon learned that sitting at the front was not a privilege. When any of her classmates misbehaved or even made a foolish mistake in their lessons, the teacher used Mi Yun as the scapegoat, striking her on the legs, hands, or even her head with a bamboo stick, showing all of the children what would happen to them if they could not do better.

Mi Yun didn't understand why she was treated differently from the other children. Her teacher didn't call her a tougee, but Mi Yun was sure that when he looked at her, he saw one.

Mi Yun favored her left hand for eating, playing games, and even washing diapers. So it made sense to her to pick up the pencil with her left hand as well.

"Mi Yun!" shouted her teacher. "You must never use that hand to write. You will bring dishonor to my classroom!"

Mi Yun found that she was always under his watchful gaze. Her left hand was struck with the bamboo stick every time she used it to lift a pencil. Some days she would return to the orphanage with red welts.

I must use my right hand, she would remind herself. *Mi Yun, don't pick up the pencil with your left hand. You must not bring dishonor to your teacher.*

On one of her first days at school, Mi Yun needed to use the outhouse during recess. As she approached the latrine, three boys stepped in front of her.

"Tougee, you can't go in. You will make it worse smelling than it is already. You are a pig. You will contaminate it for the rest of us."

Mi Yun turned and ran back to the courtyard. From that day on, she remembered to use the outhouse at the orphanage before she left for school. Then she would wait all day long, until she returned to the orphanage, to go to the bathroom again.

At the end of each school day, Mi Yun, being the tougee, was singled out to clean the hallway. Her teacher issued her a bucket of water and a rag. Getting down on her hands and knees, Mi Yun scrubbed and scoured the floors until her teacher was satisfied.

By the time she finished, the other children had already

gone home. She ran by herself back to the orphanage, where still more chores awaited her in the nursery.

I love being with the babies, she would think as she ran through the streets. *My teacher doesn't like me—but I know the babies love me.*

CHAPTER 29

Mr. and Mrs. Goliath

"Get ready, here they come!" cried one of the orphanage children as he ran into the compound from the dirt road.

Everyone in the courtyard looked up. The children had been told that an American couple would be visiting the orphanage today—and why would such a couple be coming, if not to look for a child to live with them as a servant?

Halmoni came out of the main house and stood on the step with her hands clasped behind her. "Mi Yun! Quickly! Go help prepare the babies for the American couple! They must be bathed and diapered and changed into these outfits!" She pointed to some outfits that had been stored away and brought out today, to show off the babies at their best.

Mi Yun did as she was told, then cuddled the babies and sang in their ears to keep them happy. *Halmoni will be upset with me if the babies are crying*, she thought.

In the last year, by eavesdropping on conversations among the grown-ups, Mi Yun had learned much about America. People in America received all the education needed to become wealthy. Everyone there was rich. It was a place where all one's dreams could come true. Everyone wanted to go to America.

Occasionally, one of the healthiest babies in the orphanage would be selected to go to America. This was the first time, however, that a white couple had called on the orphans in person. Mi Yun was so excited that she had the job of preparing these little ones for America.

"I'm sure they will choose you," she said to her favorite baby boy, gently pinching his cheeks. "Or maybe they will take *all* the babies to America!"

❧

The gatekeeper opened the smaller, inset door between the courtyard and the road and peeked out. He hesitated, then motioned to someone outside to wait. Closing the door and fastening it into place, he wheeled around and looked at everyone in the courtyard to make sure all was ready. Then he turned back to the metal entryway and yanked the metal posts out of their holes. With all his strength, he swung the heavy gate wide-open.

Mi Yun's jaw dropped.

She remembered the Bible story about the giant named Goliath. The little man at church had taught them that David had killed Goliath, but looking at the size of this man stepping into the courtyard, she thought that he must have surely come back to life.

This must be Goliath!

A woman who must be Mrs. Goliath followed. The two of them stopped side by side, smiling.

Lined up along the edges of the courtyard with all the

older children, Mi Yun stared at the couple from a distance. The man was the stoutest, and most certainly the tallest, man she had ever seen. Mrs. Goliath wasn't much shorter and was almost as round as her husband. Mr. Goliath's nose jutted above his huge smile, long like the noses of many of the soldiers. Although briefly distracted by the shine on the top of his head, Mi Yun was captivated by his sparkly eyes. Mrs. Goliath had a gentle face with a long nose and smooth white skin.

Only wealthy people could buy enough food to get this large! Not only were they the biggest people she had ever seen, she knew they must also be the richest.

What followed was quite a scene and very exciting. Halmoni came down from her step and crossed the courtyard to greet the white couple. She was dwarfed by them, but unruffled, she graciously welcomed the foreigners with a low bow, and they bowed respectfully in return.

The baskets with the babies were brought out to the courtyard.

With an interpreter by her side, Halmoni conversed with the couple. After many minutes Halmoni led them over to the baskets. Mi Yun watched uneasily as Mr. Goliath reached into a basket and lifted up her favorite baby. Mi Yun had seen much smaller men do terrible things to babies. She wanted to scream, *Don't hold the baby! You are too big. You will crush him!*

But the man placed his huge hands under the infant's head and bottom. He stretched the baby the length of his forearm and looked into his eyes. The baby's legs dangled loosely. The man's smile grew even broader. Then he gently pulled the infant close to him and tucked him under his chin, nestling the baby into his enormous neck. He stroked the baby's head and murmured softly. Tenderly placing the child back into the basket, he moved through the next several baskets, picking up the infants and cuddling them just as he had the first.

Several feet away, Mrs. Goliath bent over baskets, cooing to the babies. Intrigued, Mi Yun moved closer. It was then that she noticed tears streaming down the man's face. Why would anyone cry over a baby no one wanted?

Who *were* these people?

Mi Yun edged even closer. Mr. Goliath embraced another baby. Then, suddenly, he looked her way. Putting down the baby gently, he moved toward her. Frightened and yet captivated, Mi Yun couldn't move. Instead, she shifted her gaze to the dirt. But the man slowly crouched low to the ground, placed two fingers under Mi Yun's chin to lift her head, and looked into her eyes.

Although Mi Yun shuffled back a step to distance herself from this Goliath, he stretched out his enormous hand and caressed her cheek. Heat began to spread all over her. From the top of her head to the ends of her toes, she felt a tingle and warmth. Mi Yun couldn't pull away. She was mesmerized by his tender touch, which covered her face and neck, but even more so by the tears trickling down his face. Her heart beat loudly ... thump ... thump ... thump ... thump. *What was happening?* She was afraid Halmoni would hear the beating of her heart and get angry.

The emotions that swept over Mi Yun were raw and confusing. The white Swedish lady and the nurses at the clinic had been kind to her. The orphans who had included her in their little girls' secrets and games had lessened the loneliness she felt. But this touch was different from anything she had felt in a long, long time.

Mi Yun longed to say, *Please don't take your hand away. This feels good. This feels right.*

But years of self-preservation had taught Mi Yun not to trust such feelings, so she reacted in the only way she knew.

She yanked his hand from her face and spat on him.

A shocked hush fell over the courtyard. Mi Yun braced herself for punishment from the huge white man.

Goliath remained and returned her flashing glare with an intense but tender gaze.

What is wrong with this giant? Why doesn't he hit me? Mi Yun defiantly glowered at him, her expression challenging him to slap her.

Instead, his eyes were filled with a kindness she couldn't comprehend. Slowly rising, he patted Mi Yun gently on the shoulder and moved in the direction of Mrs. Goliath, who had been watching intently. After exchanging words with the interpreter and Halmoni, Mr. and Mrs. Goliath walked out the gate of the orphanage courtyard. Halmoni turned, crossed the courtyard, and disappeared into her quarters. The children were dismissed.

Mi Yun knew that she would soon reap Halmoni's wrath. The couple had left with no baby.

❦

For the rest of the day, Mi Yun waited to receive her lashes. But there was no punishment. None of the workers acknowledged what had happened. There weren't even whispers among her roommates that night.

Mi Yun fell asleep, certain that morning would bring punishment. *Maybe I will be sent away from the orphanage,* she thought.

Fitfully, she dreamt. From out of the shadows, Mr. Goliath came toward her with his outstretched hand. When he drew near, she spat on him, again and again and again. Startled awake, she scolded herself with a heavy heart.

Why did I spit on him? I don't want to live on the streets again.

CHAPTER 30

The New Dress

The green gate of Halmoni's orphanage clanged shut behind David and Judy Merwin. They walked in silence along the dusty road for several minutes.

The Merwins desperately wanted a child. David had grown up in a large family, with much laughter and companionship from many brothers and sisters. Having been raised with only a father and brother, Judy was captivated by the Merwin clan and had hoped for such a family. But they had been married for nearly ten years and had been unable to conceive. As new missionaries in South Korea, they had been overwhelmed by the magnitude of the needs in the war-torn nation. But nothing had touched their hearts more than the thousands of parentless children scattered across the country.

They had been in South Korea only six months when the American government had granted permission for American citizens to adopt Korean children, in an effort to help rebuild the devastated country. The Merwins believed that God would clearly draw each of their hearts to the same *orphan who needed parents. While they were open to any child, David especially wanted a baby boy and had already chosen the name Stephen. They had visited several orphanages in search of their baby. But there had never been a sense of peace about any particular child at any of them, confirming that they were to bring that child into their family. After every orphanage visit, they left empty-handed.*

"So, Dave, what did you think?" asked Judy, as they walked away after their visit to Halmoni's orphanage.

David was thoughtful. "They're all precious. I could take any one of them home. Each one of them needs us. There are just so many."

"Was there one you were especially drawn to—any 'Stephen?'"

David took her arm and drew her close. "I did feel drawn to one."

"A Stephen?"

David stopped and looked at his wife, his eyes brimming with tears. He could hardly find the words to speak. "No. I didn't find Stephen."

Judy hesitated, then said, "The little girl you knelt by— the one who spat at you. Is she the one?"

All David could do was to gently nod his head.

The young couple talked and prayed deep into the night. This little girl was older than they had anticipated for an adopted child, and they recognized the signs of an abusive past. After all, she had spat on David! Were they prepared to raise such a child? Maybe they just needed some sleep. Maybe, by morning, the impulse would pass.

Morning came … and they knew.

⇥⇤

Late in the afternoon on the day after Mi Yun's disgrace with the foreign Goliath in the courtyard, Mi Yun heard a commotion as she worked in the nursery and rushed to the doorway. The gatekeeper, clearly excited, was running across the courtyard to yell at Halmoni's building, "The foreigners are back! The foreigners are back!" Then he scurried back to the gate and swung it open. The foreign couple stepped inside.

Children began to emerge from different corners of the compound.

Mi Yun's tummy did a somersault. *Why are they back? They must be angry! They must want Halmoni to punish me!*

She watched them through a crack in the door as they disappeared into Halmoni's office. A few moments later, one of the older orphans ran hollering into the baby section. "Mi Yun—Halmoni wants to see you right away!"

Trembling, Mi Yun knew she needed to obey. What she wanted was to run away, but she had nowhere to go. As slowly as possible, Mi Yun finished diapering a baby. Heart hammering, she trudged to Halmoni's quarters and softly knocked.

"Come in!" Halmoni called.

After sliding the door open in slow motion, Mi Yun stepped into the room. Halmoni sat behind her desk, facing an interpreter and Mr. and Mrs. Goliath, both of whom were perched awkwardly on the floor across from her. Mi Yun was momentarily distracted by Mrs. Goliath's white legs, which stretched straight out in front of her. No one sat like that!

Halmoni motioned for the child to approach. Mi Yun dutifully inched toward the desk, bowed, and waited. Halmoni sternly scrutinized Mi Yun, then she pointed emphatically at the foreign couple and said, "Mi Yun, this American man and woman are going to take you to their home. This is a great honor. You will need to be a very, very good girl. If you are not, they will bring you back. If you thought things were difficult for you before, your life will be very hard if you return."

Mi Yun was confused. Why would they be taking me? Was Mr. Goliath going to punish me? She didn't understand why else she would be asked to leave the orphanage. Panic swept through her. *If I'm to be punished, why can't Halmoni punish me right here?* Other than the clinic, the orphanage was by far the nicest place Mi Yun had lived since leaving her mother, and now she was being asked to leave it behind.

Mrs. Goliath hunched at her waist, pushed herself up off the floor, and stood. Halmoni, Mr. Goliath, and the interpreter watched as she moved toward Mi Yun and held out her hand. Mi Yun fearfully glanced at Halmoni, who nodded her head and motioned Mi Yun to follow the white woman.

Mi Yun apprehensively took the woman's hand. Together they stepped into a side room and slid the paper door closed behind them. Mrs. Goliath held a bundle under her arm, neatly wrapped in newspaper. She unrolled the paper to reveal a pink dress with white polka-dots.

Mi Yun stared greedily. It was the most beautiful dress she had ever seen! Mrs. Goliath draped it over her arm and leaned toward the child. As she reached for the bottom edge of the coarse school shirt, Mi Yun quickly stepped back in confusion. But the woman spoke tenderly in words Mi Yun could not understand as she held up the dress.

Mi Yun remembered all of the people who had hurt her, who had taken advantage of her. But then she thought, *Halmoni sent me in here with Mrs. Goliath, and she seems kind—I think it must be okay. I don't think she'll hurt me. And look at this pretty dress. It's the prettiest dress in the world.*

Hesitantly, she let Mrs. Goliath remove her blouse and skirt.

Carefully, Mrs. Goliath helped Mi Yun step into a soft white garment that fit snugly next to her skin, around her waist and bottom. Mi Yun would learn later that this was underwear, something she had never worn or even heard of before. Then the polka-dotted dress was pulled over her head, and the pink straps were tied in bows on top of her bony shoulders.

Why am I being dressed in such a pretty dress? she wondered.

A smiling Mrs. Goliath clapped her hands together. Mi Yun felt as if she were in a dream. The white woman again held out her hand. This time Mi Yun hesitated for just a moment before holding out her own. Together they joined the others in Halmoni's office.

Mr. Goliath's face brightened, and his eyes began to twinkle. By now, Mi Yun was thoroughly confused. Her thoughts tumbled. *Maybe I am going to be a servant in an American house. I will be scrubbing their floors, as I scrub the floor at school, and cleaning their dishes and washing their laundry. It will be better than life in the orphanage. Look what nice clothes they give even to their servants!*

By the time the group reappeared on the porch, the courtyard had filled with children and the orphanage workers. Mi Yun looked up at Halmoni, who was wiping her eyes with a handkerchief. Some of the other workers had tears in their eyes too. Someone nearby whispered that she would be going to America, where everyone is rich. *Was this true?* Mi Yun understood none of this. But she felt very special in her new dress.

While Mr. and Mrs. Goliath were saying their good-byes to Halmoni, the orphanage girls surrounded Mi Yun and began touching the pink dress. She recognized envy in their eyes. She remembered how she felt every time a baby in the orphanage was sent away to new parents. Although her heart had ached with the knowledge that she would never again see that child, she had also felt excitement over their good fortune, and though she had not thought it possible, she had always longed to be chosen herself. Now she had been chosen ... even if only as a servant.

Mr. and Mrs. Goliath each clasped one of Mi Yun's hands and started toward the orphanage gate. The other children followed, crowding one another and pressing into her. The gatekeeper politely bowed as they stepped past him out onto the bustling road. Secure in the tight grips of Mr. and Mrs. Goliath, Mi Yun slowly turned her head and looked back. The orphans were waving good-bye.

CHAPTER 31

All Things New

Where this strange couple was taking her remained a mystery. During the long walk, they spoke with one another in a language Mi Yun did not understand. Mi Yun rehearsed Halmoni's instructions in her mind. *Be good ... very good. If I'm not good, they will take me back to the orphanage. I must do everything these giants tell me to do.*

They walked to the edge of the bustling city and beyond, into the countryside. Mi Yun looked ahead to the gently rolling mountains in front of her, for much of her life the only home she had known. Fields of lush, deep-green rice stalks swayed softly in the breeze. Even though it had been cruel to her, she loved this countryside and felt a peace inside as she walked along, holding hands with this couple.

Who are these people? What will they do with me? she wondered. *What if this turns out to be even worse than the orphanage? Should I try to escape now, before I am trapped?* But the touch of their hands was both firm and gentle, and their eyes were so warm.

She remembered the man's touch against her cheek,

and the way the woman had looked at her, so happy, when she presented Mi Yun with the new dress. These people seemed kind and good.

I will wait and see what happens, Mi Yun thought.

Startled back to reality by shouting voices up ahead, Mi Yun looked up to see a group of children running toward them. She felt a surge of panic, remembering the way she had often been mistreated even by children when she had been on her own, not far from here. *Oh no! They are coming after me. I must run!*

She tried to tug her hand out of the giants' grasp, pulling backward away from the approaching crowd. The woman paused, looking down at Mi Yun, and smiled at her tenderly. Mi Yun's heart continued to pound, but for some reason she trusted this large woman. She wrapped her arms around the legs of the giant and held tightly. Mrs. Goliath would protect her.

To Mi Yun's surprise, Mr. Goliath began speaking to the approaching children in broken Korean. Although his accent was funny and his words very choppy, she understood him.

"*An-yong, an-yong!* Hello," he called to the children.

"*Hwan-yong-ham-ni-da!* Welcome back," they replied.

Who are these children? wondered Mi Yun. *Do these Americans have more children who work for them? Maybe I should run away!* she thought again.

By now the group of children was standing directly in front of Mi Yun. Mi Yun was very confused—why were they all smiling at her? Hadn't they come to bother her?

"*An-yong,*" one said to her.

Mi Yun did not answer.

"*An-yong,*" said another. "My name is Jin Kyong. *Ban-gap-sup-nee-da.* Nice to meet you."

The giants continued their journey, again with each of them holding one of Mi Yun's hands, and the children walked alongside. Some of the younger children began reaching for the giants' hands, and Mi Yun tightened her grip. She felt a little angry at these children but didn't really know why. They seemed so carefree, chatting in Korean among themselves about Mi Yun and the American couple.

"Look at her eyes," one exclaimed. "They are so pretty."

Pretty? Mi Yun felt warm inside. No one besides her mother had ever told her she was pretty. Why were these children being so friendly to her?

A few of the boys walked behind Mrs. Goliath. They began chanting, "Look at the lady's bottom! She has such a big bottom!"

Horrified, Mi Yun looked up at Mrs. Goliath. Her response to the boys' chant was simply a big smile! Mi Yun's grip loosened, and she felt a grin spread across her face. Mi Yun was fascinated by the high spirits and laughter as they walked through the rice fields.

A farmer paused from his work in the field. "Welcome home, Missionary Merwin. Did you have a good trip?"

Although the giant man spoke very little Korean and the farmer little English, the two men paused for a short conversation conveyed mostly in smiles and gestures and nods. Then they continued on. They passed through a burial ground, and then the path led them through a grove of towering green trees. The path was darker beneath the trees, and Mi Yun felt a chill.

One of the boys said, "This pine forest belongs to my family. My family harvests pine nuts."

Oh, my—his family owns a whole grove of trees? This boy must be rich, thought Mi Yun. As they escaped the eeriness of the forest, Mi Yun looked ahead and noticed a gate similar to the one at the orphanage. *Oh, no.* Her heart sank. *Another orphanage!*

Mi Yun pulled back. But when she saw no fear on the faces of the other children, she continued on to see what was on the other side.

At the gate, the giant man reached up and pulled on a rope, and a loud bell rang.

The gate opened, revealing the wrinkled, grinning face of a man. He greeted the American couple with many bows. "*Hwan-yong-ham-ni-da. Hwan-yong-ham-ni-da.* Welcome home. Welcome home."

These people seemed more happy than anyone else she had ever met.

They walked through the gate into a large, open, gravelly courtyard. The grounds were well cared for—lush plants and beautiful flowers grew all around. A flagpole stood in the center, and beyond that, a church building. A collection of buildings, large and small, were scattered around the outside edges of the courtyard. This looked nothing like the orphanage.

"This is a college," one of the older boys explained.

"What is a college?"

"A school for the educated ones. Everyone here is very smart."

Many people waved at the Americans. Mi Yun could tell that Mr. and Mrs. Goliath were well liked by these people.

"*Anyeonoseyo. Anyeonoseyo.* Welcome back. Welcome back," they called out.

"*Kam-sa-ham-ni-da.* Thank you. Thank you," Mr. Goliath called.

Once the greetings had been given, most of the children withdrew back out the gate, and the rest made their way along a well-worn path to the far side of the compound, where they disappeared into a cluster of smaller buildings. Alone again with the American couple, Mi Yun followed them through the courtyard and up a small grassy hill to a yellow building with glistening red tiles on the roof. The wooden door was painted green.

It is so pretty. Look at the yellow ... it's like the sun. And the red roof. And look! There is glass on the windows, just like at the nurses' home! They must be so rich.

Mi Yun was standing in wonder, taking in these new sights, when she felt a gentle push on her back. The door was opened and a young Korean woman welcomed them. "*Anyeonoseyo.*"

Mi Yun could tell that this girl worked here. *She will be the one to teach me how to work for these people. She seems kind.*

Mi Yun stepped into a small foyer and took off her rubber shoes.

"My name is Soon Bok," the young woman said, "but you can call me *Eon-ni*—Big Sister. Welcome to the missionary house. I help the Americans here in their home. This must be very different for you." Her smile broadened. "I know that the missionary lady doesn't speak Korean. And the man knows very little. But they are very caring. They are so happy to have you here. You are very lucky to live here. Come with me."

Soon Bok gestured, and Mi Yun followed her to the kitchen. It was like none Mi Yun had seen before—in fact, she did not know what all of these big shiny things were. With pride, Soon Bok stepped up to a shiny white box, bigger than Mi Yun, and twisted a knob on the top. Mi Yun jumped in astonishment as flames shot into the air.

Soon Bok giggled. "Yes, the first time the missionary lady showed me, I was scared too."

Looking very pleased, Mrs. Goliath stood beside a taller, narrower white box with a hinged door. She pulled on the handle and opened the door.

Mi Yun's eyes widened. *Look at all those eggs! And fruits and vegetables! Who are these people? Only rich people could have so many eggs!*

Next to the kitchen was a small room with what appeared to be a table, but it was so tall! Mi Yun had always sat on the floor before a low table to eat. Mrs. Goliath stepped up to the table and sat next to it on a board held up by four sticks. Her legs hung down and tucked beneath the board.

"These are called chairs," Soon Bok explained with a smile.

Mi Yun was starting to feel tired from so many changes, so many new experiences in such a short time, but she followed Soon Bok through a sliding door into another room. In the middle of this room was a large square object with blankets spread neatly on top. Four short, fat sticks held it up off the floor. Mrs. Goliath lay down on top of it. Patting it gently, she said a word Mi Yun did not understand: "Bed."

Pointing to a smaller version of this square object over in the corner, she continued, "*Your* bed."

Mi Yun looked at Soon Bok in confusion. The older girl said, "You will sleep here. You must eat and have a bath before you can sleep. I have prepared the evening meal."

Not until Soon Bok spoke of food did Mi Yun realize how hungry she was!

Back in the room with the tall table, the white man pulled out a chair and gestured for Mi Yun to climb up onto it.

How do I get up there? Mi Yun wondered. She backed up to the chair and stood on her tiptoes. The seat hit the middle of her back. She looked up at the white man and frowned. Smiling, he leaned over to lift Mi Yun. She let him place her on the board. The man sat on the chair next to her, while his wife sat across the table from Mi Yun.

Soon Bok returned with a large plate of food, which she placed on the table before them. When she went back into the kitchen, Mr. Goliath bowed his head and prayed.

Mi Yun took her first bite of the food placed in front of her.

Oh my—what is this?

It was like nothing she had tasted before. It was noodles

with red sauce on top, but it was not spicy-hot with red pepper, as Mi Yun was used to.

Yum! Mi Yun loved the taste.

She devoured all that was on her plate. Mrs. Goliath dished up another helping for Mi Yun, and she ate that too!

Did this mean she could eat as much as she wanted? She had never been allowed to eat more than a single serving.

Her brain said *eat*, but her tummy felt like it might pop.

The American woman stood, looked at Mi Yun, and said a few words. Then she walked away into a different room and shut the door. Wondering what the woman had said, Mi Yun continued to sit at the table. She could hear the sound of water running in the room Mrs. Goliath had gone into, and steam began seeping out from beneath the door. Then Mrs. Goliath poked her head out the door and motioned for Mi Yun to come.

Mi Yun had experienced so many new things this day, she really just wanted to go to a hidden corner somewhere and close her eyes. But she remembered Halmoni's words. She slid off the chair and entered the steamy room.

There was a large wooden tub with hot water bubbling into it.

But when Mrs. Goliath started to unfasten the pretty dress that Mi Yun had been given earlier that day, she wrapped her arms around herself and pulled away. Mrs. Goliath tried again to unfasten the dress. Mi Yun shook her head.

Mrs. Goliath called out through the door, and soon Mi Yun heard the patter of Soon Bok's feet in the hallway. As soon as Soon Bok appeared in the doorway, Mi Yun cried,

"Eonni, she wants to take my dress away! Please don't let her take it away!"

"Don't be afraid, Mi Yun. She will give it back. She just wants to wash you."

Reassured, Mi Yun allowed herself to be undressed. The white lady lifted her off the cold floor and gently placed her into the water. Mi Yun closed her eyes. *What is this? It stings, but the warmth feels so good.* Never before had Mi Yun been immersed in a hot bath!

Exhausted, Mi Yun relaxed into the soothing water. Her eyes became heavy. *I could stay here forever*, she thought.

But before she could fall asleep, the American woman lifted her to a standing position in the tub. Mi Yun was so relaxed she was limp, but she found her footing on the bottom of the slick wood. Then, with a brush, Mrs. Goliath started scrubbing Mi Yun.

Mi Yun wanted to cry from the pain of the rough brush, but she held back her tears.

The American woman scrubbed, and scrubbed, and scrubbed some more. Mi Yun did not know what she was saying, but she shouted as she scrubbed.

Soon Bok was still in the room. "What is she shouting?" Mi Yun asked.

Soon Bok giggled. "She is telling the American man you are so dirty! Look at all the dirt in the water—it is brown! She says it will take two or three baths to get the dirt off you! But don't worry—only one bath tonight."

Mrs. Goliath held Mi Yun's wet hair out from her head and squinted at it. After looking at it in several places, she shouted again.

Soon Bok said, "Now she is asking the missionary what they should do about the lice in your hair. She asks him, 'How much medicine do you think I should put on her head?'"

Then it was time for Soon Bok to leave for the night, so now Mi Yun had no way of knowing what the Americans were saying. The woman rubbed something sticky onto Mi Yun's head and then wrapped it with a towel. Mrs. Goliath helped Mi Yun into a different outfit, a big top with matching pants. Mi Yun watched as the woman hung Mi Yun's pretty dress on a hook on the wall. Then the woman motioned for Mi Yun to lie on her bed.

Mr. Goliath sat on her bed by her feet, and Mrs. Goliath sat near her head. Mi Yun watched as they closed their eyes and, speaking in their funny language, they prayed. Then she closed her eyes too.

CHAPTER 32

Stephanie

Mi Yun slept soundly that night. In the morning, she was awakened by sunshine streaming through the glass windows. She looked around the room. The Americans were gone; she was alone. Mi Yun wasn't sure what to do now.

Oh, I really need to find the potty, she thought. *But I don't know where it is.*

Quietly, she slipped out of bed and found the room where she had been given a bath the night before. Searching for the hole to use, she found nothing.

Maybe it is outside.

She tiptoed silently out the door, looking for an outhouse. But she found no place to relieve herself. What should she do?

The urge was getting stronger. Finally Mi Yun could hold it no longer, and she squatted beside the yellow house. She was still squatting there when she heard a giggle behind her. Startled, Mi Yun turned to see the white woman watching her, a hand covering her mouth. Mi Yun felt her cheeks heat up and knew she was blushing.

Would she be punished? Would she be sent back to the orphanage?

But the American lady did not seem angry. She just stood smiling at Mi Yun, waiting for Mi Yun to pull up her pants. Then she took Mi Yun by the hand and led her back into the house, down the hallway, and back to the room with the bath. She went to a white chair in the corner, lifted the cover of the seat, and pointed down into it. Mi Yun warily peeked into the hole in the middle of the seat but saw nothing. The lady sat down on the seat to show Mi Yun how to use it. She made some funny noises, stood up, and pulled on a string hanging down from the ceiling. Swoosh! A rumble of water came down a pipe and filled the hole with water and then disappeared.

Oh! This is the outhouse? Where is the poop? Where is the smell?

Curious, Mi Yun reached up and pulled on the string. Water again swooshed into the big bowl and disappeared down the hole. Mi Yun was amazed. She could have spent all day flushing the toilet, but Mrs. Goliath led her gently out of the room.

⭤

Later that day, Mr. Goliath came home with a Korean man named Mr. Park. Mr. Park, Mi Yun learned later, was Mr. Goliath's interpreter.

"Hello, little girl. How are you doing?" Mr. Park said.

"Good."

"Do you like it here?"

"Oh, yes. I have a really pretty dress."

"These Americans would like to give you an American name."

"I already have a name," Mi Yun said uneasily. This was not good news. *I really like Mi Yun, and it means "Beautiful Dawn."*

"They want to call you Stephanie. Stephanie," he repeated. "This name means, 'The Crowned One.'"

That sounds nice too—but it is not as pretty as Mi Yun.

"Can you say, Stef-a-nee?" Mr. Park asked. "Go ahead."

"Suh-te-fu-nee?" she tried.

"Yes! Very good!" he said. "Stephanie Merwin."

"Mo-o-won?"

"Good! That's right! Stephanie Merwin."

"Suh-te-fu-nee," she said again. *American names are really hard. Why doesn't Eonni have an American name?*

Mi Yun turned to the Merwins and pointed to herself, saying, "Suh-te-fu-nee."

"Yes, that's your new name—Stephanie." They both smiled at her. "Stephanie."

"Okay. Suh-te-fu-nee." She forced a smile in return.

⋟⋞

Over the next several days, Stephanie learned many new things and ate very well. She hadn't known that there were so many different kinds of foods: noodles, vegetables, red meat, white meat, eggs, fruits. She never went hungry.

These foreigners loved their baths, and she did too! Each night before climbing into bed she sat in the warm tub of water and was scrubbed by Mrs. Merwin. Each night, she left behind more of the caked-on dirt that had covered her body for almost as long as she could remember.

She was not happy when her head was shaved—they told her it was the only way to get rid of the lice nesting in it. But no one laughed at her bald head.

At the new school she began attending, the teachers and other children always acknowledged her with greetings. The children in the neighborhood wanted to play with her, and the candy store man gave her candy. No more stealing! These people were kind.

Stephanie felt safe when the Americans prayed each night as they put her to bed, but she pulled away if they leaned too close to hug or kiss her.

Several weeks passed.

⋇

One morning Stephanie was helping Eonni wash clothes in the front yard.

"When will the hard work start for me?" she asked

Eonni laughed. "You will not have to work hard. This is your home. Just be a good girl."

Stephanie did not understand, but she didn't ask any more questions about working here.

⋇

A few days later, Stephanie wandered into the college girls' dorm.

"I smell an American!" one of the girls called in Korean.

Stephanie looked around. "No—there is no American here," she replied.

"I smell cheese, and only Americans eat cheese! You are the American! You are American now."

What was this girl talking about?

"Your new name is Stephanie," the girl explained. "You have an American family now."

Yes, it was true that Mi Yun was called Suh-te-fu-nee by the American couple. Yes, she ate American food—sometimes cheese. Yes, the white man and his wife were very kind to her—but she wasn't part of their family. "No, I am not an American. I am just their servant," Stephanie argued.

The older girl burst out laughing. "No, you silly! You belong to them! They are your mommy and daddy now. They adopted you."

Stephanie stood motionless, shocked and confused. What was this girl saying? She ran out of the dormitory, up the hill, and burst into her new home.

Adopted? What is that? What does she mean I have a family? A mommy and daddy? Stephanie sat in a quiet corner to think through these new thoughts. *Does this mean these people want me to live with them ... forever? That I never have to leave? That I will never be cold or hungry again? That they chose ugly me?*

How could this be? It seemed impossible that the tougee, the orphan girl who had been tied to the waterwheel, who had been thrown down the well, who had been left for the rats to eat, should now be chosen by a family that loves her. *Adopted.* She did not understand the word. But the college girl had said, "They are your mommy and daddy now." Stephanie understood that. *Could it be true?* She thought of the smiles on the faces of the American couple when they looked at her. Of the way they knelt and prayed with her at bedtime. Of the joy with which they handed her an abundance of food, more food than she had ever had before, day after day. She thought of the pretty pink dress and the woman's face as she had given it to Stephanie.

She still did not understand. But she felt something light ... something new ... in her heart.

Citizenship

Stephanie adapted to her new world and learned to pronounce and answer to her new name. She delighted in her new identity as the American missionaries' daughter. She eagerly exchanged Korean for English and attended a missionary school with children of other missionaries. Her parents took her to a number of doctors to rid her of worms, boils, scabs, and infected wounds. Her body healed, and her skin became healthy before her very eyes.

Stephanie visited one particular doctor over and over again. Each time it was the same routine. She took deep breaths while he listened to her chest through a tube. He inspected her skin, teeth, and head, poked around a bit, and said, "I can tell you are getting better every time you come. Now come with me, and let's take your pictures." The pictures he took were always of her chest. She never got to see them, but the pictures she saw on his walls were all of just bones.

Stephanie's parents adopted another child about a year after Stephanie was chosen from the orphanage—a ten-pound, one-year-old girl not yet able to sit up on her own.

Stephanie enjoyed several long journeys into Seoul with her parents. They took her to a building filled with many other Americans. As she sat for what seemed like hours, waiting patiently for her parents to finish speaking with some man who must be important, she counted the stars on the American flag. She studied the soldiers who stood at attention, eyes looking straight ahead, and wondered how they stood still for such a long time.

Stephanie knew, because her parents had told her, that they were talking to the important man about taking her to visit America. She didn't know where America was, but she was sure it would be an adventure. She was told that the only things left to wait for were her pictures. They had to turn out just right before she would be allowed to travel.

When I get to America, I will never tell anyone about the streets. I will never be a tougee again, *she vowed.*

Nobody needed to know about her life before her adoption. She was Stephanie Anne Merwin now. She had even been given a birthday.

✢

Three years after Stephanie walked out of the orphanage holding onto the hands of Mr. and Mrs. Goliath, she stood in front of a district judge in Chicago, Illinois, the United States of America. Traveling for days over the Pacific Ocean and then by land to the Midwest had taken, it seemed to Stephanie, an eternity. Now she was being sworn in as an American citizen, along with hundreds of others from around the world.

Stephanie and her sister—who was now a bubbly

four-year-old and excited by this big party—would be the youngest to receive their papers of citizenship this day. Many photographers and journalists had come to document this event. After Stephanie and her sister had raised their hands and sworn an oath of allegiance along with the hundreds of others, the judge pointed to Stephanie and motioned with his finger for her to come up to where he was.

Stephanie became very afraid. *Could I have done something wrong? I thought that I answered all the questions right. I studied so hard!* Was the judge going to send her back to Korea, back to the orphanage? She looked anxiously up at her dad. He nodded reassuringly and gave her a nudge toward the judge. Slowly, she wound through the quiet crowd, stopping just below his immense wooden bench.

"Come up here, little girl," he said, smiling.

His smile eased her fears only a little, but Stephanie climbed the few steps until she stood next to the judge. She looked toward her family standing below. Her parents were smiling, and her little sister was waving like she was at a festival. She wanted to run back to her daddy, where she felt safe. Suddenly an arm wrapped across the back of her shoulders, and Stephanie jumped back. But with a quick, gentle squeeze, the judge reassured her.

"Little girl, what is your name?"

"My name is Stephanie Anne Merwin."

"What was your name before you were adopted?"

"I don't know what name my mother gave me. In the orphanage I was called Mi Yun."

"What country did you belong to before today?"

"I was born in Korea, but I was not a citizen of Korea."

The judge scrunched his forehead. "Why?"

"I had no family who claimed me by giving me their family name. Also ... " She paused, then continued, her voice barely audible so that only the judge could hear. "I am mixed-blood."

Looking intently into Stephanie's eyes for a moment, the judge turned and addressed the crowd, his voice booming in the courtroom. "Today, it's my pleasure to introduce Stephanie Anne Merwin. She belongs to us now. To America. She will always have a family, a name, and a country. Welcome, Stephanie Anne Merwin!" The judge picked up a scroll from the table in front of him. "This document is proof that you belong." And he handed her the scroll.

Stephanie beheld the tightly rolled scroll with wonder. So focused was she on the document, she was only vaguely aware that cameras were flashing, that the room had erupted into cries of congratulation, for Stephanie and for each other, and that her tiny sister had begun to sing, "Oh, God Is Good" at the top of her voice. Stephanie unrolled her piece of paper. Emblazoned across the top were the words:

Stephanie Anne Merwin
Naturalized Citizen of the United States of America

She looked up at her mommy and daddy; they were crying and laughing all at once, hugging total strangers. Daddy rushed to Stephanie, lifted her into the air, and swung her around. Stephanie didn't even try to pull away.

She embraced this moment. Her dream had come true. Now she knew that she belonged forever to this giant of a man and his loving wife.

She was finally home.

Home!

An Open Letter
from the Author

Thank you for allowing me to tell this story of survival and redemption. I've had the privilege of sharing my experiences domestically and internationally for over thirty years. No matter where I go, orphans and adoptees come up to me and say, "You are telling my story too!" The details of our lives may differ—I realize that I may be the only one, and most likely the only five year old—who followed train tracks in an attempt to find my mother. But whatever the circumstances, the emotional scarring is always recognizable. We all share the same pain of rejection, betrayal, and abuse. My story is simply one among millions.

Sadly, most orphans across the planet do not get the opportunity to share their stories, much less start the healing process necessary for them to experience how joyful and rewarding life can truly be. I often remember with great sadness the boy I wrote about whose life had become so difficult that he threw himself into the fire. I believe that our lives are meant to be a gift, not a burden.

The media exposes the nightmare that life has become

for so many children. We see and hear evidence of a brutal world filled with child slavery, child abandonment, children left on garbage heaps. The examples are infinite. It might be a child slave in Haiti, or one trafficked into the sex trade of Addis Ababa, Ethiopia. It might be a child passing through the train station in Delhi, India, en route to a life of forced domestic service, or one living on the streets in Brazil or one of the Baltic nations. Orphans are everywhere. Young boys and girls are being pimped in New York City, suffering in sweatshops in impoverished circumstances in many lands to meet the consumer needs of the Western world, or roaming the alleys and streets of countless cities trying to find food.

Nearly all of us believe that each child deserves to be loved and cherished, with a destiny of hope for her future. But paying lip service to that belief does nothing to right the terrible wrongs children face worldwide. My goal for every orphan is that they actually get the opportunity to have a family and a safe community where they are accepted, where they feel that they belong.

At this moment, there are an estimated 143 million orphans throughout the world who have been abandoned or abused. All are crying out for a caring person to deliver them from the hands of their oppressors. I hope my story will bear witness to the tremendous impact just one person can have on this crisis. Those advocates who are working to reverse our global orphan crisis, even one life at a time, are my real-life heroes. They are bringing justice to each Yoon Myoung and Mi Yun.

For the first twenty years of my new life, I held my

orphan story close to my heart because of the shame I felt and my fear of being rejected again. Now I share the pain, abuse, sadness, tragedy, and heartache I endured in my early years. I do it to encourage others to speak up, and to let them know they are not alone. More importantly, I want to make it clear that in every instance of my life, whether I knew it or not, there was a greater, higher, wiser power propelling willing hearts to rescue me.

Whether it was the simple village woman who allowed me to sleep in her kitchen, the old woman who pulled me from the well, the man who saved me from certain drowning at the waterwheel, the Swedish nurse at the garbage heap, or my parents who took me from the orphanage and adopted me, my rescuers were regular people who acknowledged and yielded to a divine prompting. Each may offer a different explanation of what motivated them. Whether it was simple intuition or an inner still, small voice, each willing heart heard a call for justice and exhibited grace in their reply.

I was fortunate to be born at a time when compassionate people had begun to reach out globally to the poor. Before the 1950s, there were few humanitarian organizations. The Korean conflict prompted the growth of not-for-profit non-governmental organizations (NGOs) as well as faith-based groups interested in responding to humanitarian needs. Around the time I was born, Western minds were beginning to recognize the importance of charitable acts. I am where I am today—indeed, I am *alive* today—because of that very movement. If my story inspires someone to act to promote justice, to whatever degree, then I am content in the knowledge that other orphans will be rescued.

As a global advocate for orphans, I am committed to increasing public awareness of their plight and helping to raise the funds necessary to provide permanent, secure homes for these children. There are many levels of orphan care. Many organizations run wide—but few run deep. After the initial rescue, it takes continued support to nurture a child to the point that their life has sustainability and the promise of a future. Many will never be adopted.

I passionately believe that these orphans need support in three areas. First, it is necessary to provide permanent homes for children. Most institutions, after a certain period of time, reach a stage in their relationship with their children called a "phase out"—meaning that the rescued minors are sent back into the world to fend for themselves. In many cases, those "phased out" children have not gained the physical or emotional preparation they need for the hard life ahead of them, and the next cycle of neglect begins.

And that prompts my second area of concern: rescuing young women from a life in the sex trade. Regardless of what we label these young women, most are in this predicament through no choice of their own. Most come from extreme poverty, neglect, and abuse. Many were treated brutally and sold into the trade, while others, including many "phased out" minors, are there because they have no other options: it is prostitution or starvation. As an advocate, I partner with others to mentor these women, train them for alternative jobs, and provide childcare for their children. My intent is to make viable their long-term survival.

Finally, I am committed to addressing the injustice taking place today in North Korea. There is a silent exchange between sex brokers in China and those in North Korea. Because of the extreme conditions in North Korea, many young women are desperate to leave their country. This makes them vulnerable to the lure of brokers who, promising a better life in China, convince them to flee. Once they arrive, these women, to their horror, find themselves forced into the sex trade or sold into slavery to Chinese farmers. They cannot turn back—they have nowhere to go. These captives are illegals. Without proper documentation, they and their children, who are bi-racial, are without a country and without a birthright. It has become a hidden orphan crisis.

Some of these brave women do eventually connect with organizations that try to help them escape. But to reach safety and freedom, they must go underground and endure weeks or months of grueling travel—alone, without their children. You can—imagine the plight of their deserted children. So far my efforts have focused on connecting these young women with humanitarian organizations that can help them. I am also working to bring their situation and that of their abandoned children into the light.

My gratitude for my own rescue is profound. Fortunately, I have come to know the One who compelled those willing hearts of my past to both help me personally and to, with God's grace, extend themselves to work for the cause of the orphan and the unwanted. My faith in the One has allowed me to "dump the garbage" from my past and embrace the here and now.

We have so many names for the Divine: Pure Light, Sustaining Life, Perfect Truth, the Creator. I know Him simply as Jesus, the One who has treasured me and delighted in me since before my first breath. He is the One who declared to all He chose to help me in my time of need, "She is destined for infinitely more." This is the One who continually and inexhaustibly creates beauty out of the ashen remains of my past.

And that transformation is what propels me into action on behalf of other orphans. It has taken many, many years of healing, but now I know the truth of who I am. I walk with patience, doing my part to improve orphan care. Embracing life day by day, I live with the belief that *great things lie ahead*.

Although this written account ends when I was twelve years old, I have now come to a place in my life where I can say with all conviction: There is nothing that has happened to me that I would have been better off without. How I came to this milestone in my journey, this place of acceptance, is another story. It is one that I will tell, with openness and complete honesty, in my next book: *Spirit of Mine—Living Beyond Survival*. Please look for it on my website, *www.stephaniefast.org*

With love and blessings,
STEPHANIE FAST